Let The Trumpets Sound!
(Handel's Messiah)

The Autobiography of James Winder
1922-1981

Introduction
NOW SOUND THE TRUMPETS

As most of my life has been connected with music – and especially Military music, I thought the title was appropriate to the following narrative.

If the sounding of trumpets was the prelude to dashing deeds of unimaginable bravery and heroism on my part – forget it. This story is about a humble person who was no braver than the rest – and in fact a lot less braver than the average. The fact is, we all have a story to tell, but most people lack the time and / or the opportunity to do so. I have been fortunate enough to possess both.

This then is the story of my years spent in the most famous Army the world has ever known – the British Army. I make no apology for this arrogant piece of boasting, because I sincerely believe it. However, this is an autobiography and not a recruiting poster, so I have continued into the post –Army years as these contained the bulk of our Far East travels.

It has been interesting to write this, and I do hope that it will be just as interesting for you to read it. As it has been compiled completely from memory (and sometimes the aid of Joyce's diaries!) there may be a few small errors here and there, but they are purely unintentional, and if you spot them – please forgive me.

I would like to dedicate this work to my very loyal and hardworking wife Joyce, who has been my main support over the years, and who has given me two extremely lovely daughters, as well as her understanding and sympathy.

Thank you Joyce.

BOOK ONE

Chapter 1
THE LOWEST OF THE LOW

All boys have an ambition – be it jet-pilot, pop star, pro footballer or what have you, and I was no exception. My favourite dream was to make a parachute drop. The thrill of standing on the wing of a trundling biplane, pulling the ripcord and feeling the 'chute flow out behind me, followed by that beautiful ghastly leap out into space (actually parachutists *did* jump that way when I was a boy!).

It all began way back in early 1938 when I noticed a recruiting poster in my native Woolwich. It showed a Guards drummer boy dressed in a magnificently braided uniform complete with bearskin, and I really fell in love with that poster – the concept, not the boy! Not having any particular prospects in civil life (does an errand boy have any?) and coming from a military family the inevitable happened – I marched smartly to the Central London Recruiting Office in Great Scotland Yard - a forbidding pile of masonry, but the gateway to great adventures (my fervent hope). After three false starts by putting my age to enlist as a private soldier, and each time being confounded by lack of a birth certificate, I finally made it by production of my real birth certificate, and a humble confession, then after a fourth medical and acceptance of the King's shilling I was formally sworn into His Majesty's Army as the lowest of the low – a bandboy. Unfortunately, the night before the great step, I saw a film at the local cinema (The Granada, Woolwich) entitles "The Lives of a Bengal Lancer" showing a scene wherein the hero was subjected to great torture – i.e. burning splints pushed under his fingernails – to make him reveal the location and strength of his regiment. This rather put me off my future military career, but it was now too late – the die was cast.

My chosen regiment – or rather the only one with vacancies for boys – was the Princess Alexander's Own Yorkshire Regiment, the 19th Foot, more commonly known as the Green Howards. The name originated in the seventeenth century when Regiments took this name from their Colonels. Then there happened to be two British Infantry Regiments with a Colonel Howard so to distinguish them apart the colour of their facings were prefixed. Ours being green gave us the name Green Howards – and the others the Buff Howards, known in later years as the Royal East Kent Regiment (the 'Buffs') – so much for Regimental history.

So it was on the 9th March 1938, in company with three fellow enthusiasts, Vic Fridd from East Grinstead, George Bland from Dagenham and Joe Sewell from Silvertown (later nicknamed 'Peanut' because he was shaped like one) I entrained for the unknown north – destination Catterick Camp.

After the longest train journey of our lives we stood shivering on that dingily lit Richmond station (Catterick didn't possess one), and on that cold windy night we wondered what we had let ourselves in for. We didn't have to wait long to find out. Out of the semi darkness loomed a large khaki figure with three stripes and a crown on his sleeve, and we received our first command in broad Yorkshire.

"Pick oop them cases and get on that trook".

We hastily complied, and clambered onto an open Bedford 15cwt truck for the three mile journey to the camp. Our great adventure had begun.

On arrival at bleak Catterick we were given a stodgy meal, and a large mug of what I thought was sweet soup but actually turned out to be Army tea. We drew blankets and a pillow from stores and slept our first night on hard folding iron cots in a barrack room in company with fifteen other young soldiers.

* *   *   *   *   *   *   *   *

Over the next few months we were to learn a lot. How to spit-polish boots and chinstraps, how to blanco white belts, to wind puttees and brush caps. The barrack square was not neglected either. On it we learned the intricacies of cane drill, forming fours, saluting on the march and a host of other complicated gyrations, everything being preceded by a lengthy and minute examination of our turnout. Apart from all this, we were taught the elements of music from a beery Band Sergeant named Blockley and nicknamed 'Bolshie', why I don't know, but obviously from a drunken incident in his Indian service.

At this time our Regiment was serving in Malta, and the boys plus a few NCOs and men, commanded by a Major Morkill were known as 'rear details', and while the 1st Battalion was overseas we were attached for all purposes to the 1st Battalion the Royal Inniskilling Fusiliers, an Irish Regiment famous more for its fighting qualities both in the field and the NAFFI beer bar. We soon integrated with the others but only after a struggle. Some would-be bully boys attempted to intimidate us, but being big for our age we soon disillusioned most of these junior Hitlers ourselves!

Life in the Army those days was hard, and discipline strict. Each morning at Reveille (0530 hrs in summer and 0630 hrs in winter) the Lance Corporal in charge of us – a one-striped tyrant, would leap from his bed almost before the buglers first strident note had faded and threw open every window to the freezing Yorkshire gales. He would then tour the room and overturn every bed where a horizontal body lay. Anybody caught in bed after Reveille would be charged, but as this was almost a physical impossibility nobody ever suffered that awful fate.

Before breakfast it was PT followed later by drill, education and the inevitable music training. For this we sat on long forms with 'Bolshie' scribbling meaningless (to us) symbols on a blackboard, and all of us endeavouring to be as witty as possible without actually breaking a military law or rousing the wrath of our loquacious professor. This could be highly amusing as nine tenths of us were Londoners with the natural Cockney sense of humour, and complete lack of regard for such a solemn occasion.

In the evenings a 'shiny parade' was held, when one selected item of kit was to be cleaned and produced by 9.30pm (2130 hours!). Three evenings a week we were allowed out of barracks, but had to be in by 2100 hrs and standing by our beds by 2130 hrs. Lights out was at 2215 hrs and the only sound permitted after this was a chorus of unmusical snores.

As bandboys we earned the magnificent sum of seven shillings a week (old money) but were only issued with three shillings on pay parade. The residue was held in abeyance as 'credits' and was used largely to offset clothing purchases, breakages, Barrack damages, and several other mysterious items. With our three shillings (termed the 'weekly insult') we were required to buy toilet necessities, blanco, etc and it left little to squander. Of course as tea was 1d a cup and Woodbines 5 for 2d we survived. Smoking however was strictly forbidden — which made most of us heavy smokers before we were sixteen!

After about four weeks service I was warned for a draft to our second Battalion — at that time in Razmak on the northwest frontier of India. I received three paralysing jabs, and issue of khaki drill tropical kit (including a magnificent sun helmet or 'topee') and twenty eight days embarkation leave. On my return to Catterick I found the draft was cancelled — I honestly didn't know whether to be happy or sad.

Now came the time for us as bandboys to be allocated an instrument. On a mild spring day we were marched over to Le Cateau lines, there to be interviewed by the bandmaster of the Queens Own Cameron Highlanders (now regrettably amalgamated with the Seaforth Highlanders to form the Queens Own Highlanders).

In the presence of a real live Warrant Officer Class 1 (Bandmaster) we all quivered. He took us one by one.

"What instrument are you interested in son?" he asked me.

"Please sir", I quavered — "the trombone".

He directed a searching look at me.

"Open your mouth".

I did so. Years earlier on a school outing to Sheerness, I had had the misfortune to break a tooth. He didn't miss this.

"Sarn't – put this boy down for oboe".

Bolshie hastily complied. In the background I heard a few sniggers from my comrades, but to my delight they were also deflected. Peanut was allocated to a B♭ bass, George Bland to a coronet and Vic Fridd to drums (he eluded this later and joined the MT as a driver). But now we had a purpose in life.

I wasn't very happy about the oboe, in fact I hardly knew what it was. Later I was destined to become a very proficient instrumentalist – broadcasting as a soloist on both radio and TV. However that is another story and many years later. But at this moment I looked upon the choice with some misgivings, and found myself banished to the ablutions (toilets), there to make the air hideous with blood curdling squawks!

Chapter 2
THE LAST DAYS OF PEACE

Sport played a major part in the pre-war Army. PT and cross country runs took place regularly, and boxing was very popular, both in the barrack room and the gymnasium. One embarrassing incident occurred in the gym one day. After the usual exercises the Cpl instructor lined us up in two ranks facing each other with sizes roughly corresponding, and supplied us with boxing gloves. We then proceeded to attack each other with great gusto but my opposite number - a tall buck-toothed lad named Lenney was a complete novice, so I had no problems. Vic Fridd, my pal, was also fortunate in this respect. Emboldened by our successes Vic and I decided to take on the instructor, a craggy Scot. But what we didn't know was that he was a former ABA champion! We made a good start, Vic going for the head and me for the body - but class told and with lightening footwork he came for me, completely ignoring Vic. Next second I was out cold on the floor, and he was taking Vic apart! We never issued any more rash challenges after that, and although, later on, I boxed as a welterweight for the Green Howards, I never did forget the humiliation.

Football was a more popular sport. Although few in number we were unwisely enrolled into the Catterick boys league. I was elected captain, and our last line of defence - goalkeeper. Having only twenty boys from which to pick a team was a big handicap (some were tiny boys and some had never kicked a ball before) but we turned out for every fixture, and played our hearts out. But the outcome was a forgone conclusion. Our first game against the West Yorkshire boys we crashed 7-0 although in the light of later matches this was almost a victory. The huge divisions of the Royal Signals could select from almost two hundred boys, and they regularly swamped us by prodigious scores. Other teams were as bad. I can remember when one home game against the brawny boys of the Royal Scots when our diminutive Peter Russell, the son of a former Green Howards Band Sergeant (and later himself to be Bandmaster of the Kings Liverpool Regiment), played the game of his life, tearing into the Scots' defence like a terrier, eventually scoring two beautiful goals, but the outcome was inevitable - we lost 15-2! And I still have a scar on my knee to remind me of this match.

Eventually the 1st Battalion Green Howards returned home from Palestine and Malta, and we occupied the new 'Belisha' barracks in Bourlon Lines. Named after the then War Minister Lord Hore-Belisha, the huge block was the last word in military luxury. Spring beds, small barrack rooms, constant hot water and central hearing with good food, were all part of the service. We now met the boys who had travelled with the Battalion - being older than us. They included Eric Thompson, an accomplished oboist (and later Bandmaster of the Norfolks) and a drummer boy named Jackson, who had earlier played football for the Army in the Middle-East (we could have used him earlier!).

We also met our Bandmaster. Reginald Lester ARCM was a small, vital man. He was a keen sportsman and a good musician but above all a strict disciplinarian (as we all found out to our cost at one time or another). He was the man we loved to hate, and we spent long hours devising a gory end for him, but in fact he outlived some of us, and after retiring from the Army became a salesman for Messrs Kitchens of Leeds - a big musical dealer. If he is still alive I should think that he is now in his seventies. Years later I visited him at Kitchens when I was a Band Sergeant in the Royal Tank Regiment. He was quite astonished to see me (as a Sergeant!) but we had a long friendly chat and I just couldn't understand why I was so scared of him in the early days. Everybody knew him as 'Chippy' - another inexplicable Army nickname.

We were glad to be with the Battalion, feeling now that we belonged somewhere instead of being batted from one Regiment to another. Even in my short service of fifteen months, we had been attached to five different Regiments - but now we were home!

1939 was a momentous year for the Green Howards. It was the 250th anniversary of the formation of the Regiment, and this was to be celebrated by a big parade involving the trooping of the Colours, and a drumhead service. Held on Alma day (one of our battle honours), the huge square was a blaze of colour. Five captured Russian drums from Alma (complete with bloodstains) were paraded in front of the band and drums, and in scarlet jacket, blue trousers and white silk gloves (specially bought in London) I felt seven feet tall as we marched around the square. Two of my enlisted comrades - George Bland and 'Peanut' Sewell were also with me (Vic Fridd had by that time joined the MT as a driver).

But the real drums of war were softly rolling on the continent of Europe. Hitler was riding high, and poor worried Chamberlain was vainly trying to secure an impossible peace. However we were not unduly worried - everyone was looking forward to war - after all it was our basic function. The death of spit and polish was eagerly awaited.

But spit and polish was not to die so easily. In August we moved out to Scampton in Yorkshire for Brigade training, but after only a fortnight we hurriedly struck camp (all through a wet and windy night) and returned to Catterick. The slow troop train journey back was painful, but not half as painful as the huge boil on the back of my neck. To relieve the boredom one of the bandsmen, with evil sadistic pleasure, squeezed out the core, much to my agony.

We now relaxed back into the luxury of Bourlon barracks, but our pleasure was short-lived. Within a few days - Sunday the third of September to be exact - Chamberlain made his historic radio speech ending with the words:

"We are now at war with Germany".

Barely five minutes later the air-raid siren screamed, and when the all clear sounded we sheepishly emerged from under our beds into six years of war.

Chapter 3
THE PHONEY WAR

The 1939-45 war began gently. After the spectacular start by a few air raids, life subsided back into the normal routine. The Battalion was moved from Bourlon barracks out into the 'exterior' darkness, namely a bleak inhospitable patch of Bellarby Moor known as Waitwith Camp. Hundreds of tents were pitched to provide accommodation for a new Infantry Brigade consisting of ourselves plus a battalion of the Durham Light Infantry and the Kings Own Yorkshire Light Infantry.

Within a few weeks the whole Brigade was ordered to France to join the growing Expeditionary Force and vanished overnight leaving behind an assortment of 'sick, lame and lazy' - in other words the 'too old, the too sick' and ourselves - 'the too young'. We, as the Brigade rear party, were then detailed to strike camp and what a monumental task that turned out to be!

Firstly we had to camouflage the tents against possible enemy air attack, and then when the faint was dry, demolish each one, carefully fold it and despatch it back to Ordinance by truck. As the total number of tents and marquees numbered well over a thousand, the whole job took us almost up to mid December 1939. We abandoned the snowy wastes of Waitwith in early December with great relief.

The next stop for the bandboys, plus a few NCOs, was a crumbling church hall in Richmond. This was also an unpopular billet as it was rat infested and having to sleep on the floor, the hideous creatures would gaily frolic around us during the night. But after vehement protests, the powers that be decreed we could move up to Richmond Barracks at the top of Gallowgate Hill - the depot of the Green Howards. This was a great improvement, although the barracks were ancient, they were solid, clean and warm and had the added advantage of being within walking distance of shops and cinemas, and staggering distance of pubs.

Christmas 1939 found us comparatively happy. No war news of any note trickled through and we celebrated in almost a peacetime atmosphere. 'Chippy' Lester was with us and in the new year one or two of the former band began to drift back (including 'Bolshie', the band sergeant) and with the aid of a dew militiamen (later to be known as national servicemen), Chippy formed a band. At first it was a pale shadow of the pre-war band but gradually as more talent flowed in, so it improved. Chippy did wonders and his musical ability, plus his organisational genius, soon made us the foremost musical unit in the whole of North Yorkshire.

But vague rumblings of militarism remained within me. In January 1940 I finished boys service and became officially know as a 'man'. This entitled me to smoke, drink and associate with women. The first two I had practiced furtively for a long time, but I disdained the third (I made up for this later!). To celebrate the event, I smoked a huge cigar during a break in morning practice, but the laugh was on me as I lurched, green-faced, to the toilets. I was still looking for a chance to get out of the band and into the Paras but Chippy was relentless and held tightly on to every musician - even the indifferent ones. To unsettle me even more I heard that my brother Charles had been promoted to sergeant, and was now on an anti-aircraft site on the south coast.

On all fronts the war was warming up. Dunkirk came and went and the subsequent fear of airborne invasion (by German paratroopers dressed as nuns - which became a standard joke) even reached North Yorkshire. Every dawn and dusk we all stood to and marched around the perimeter of the barracks complete with leather equipment, rifle and bayonet, but alas no ammunition!

The band's primary function at this time was to tour the North Riding villages endeavouring to extract money from the rich (reserved occupation) farmers. This we did fairly successfully under the guise of 'Warship Weeks', 'Wings for Victory' and 'Serve the Soldier' weeks. Such sleepy villages as Bedale, Masham, Reeth, Leyburn and a host of others turned out to see us thunder through retreat beatings and programmes of martial music, but on most occasions the band outnumbered the audience.

Back in barrack we played at a weekly concert in the same 'stone' gymnasium (one of our guest artists was Vic Oliver) and the dance band did a weekly stint in the same spot. Church parade and retreat beatings in Richmond also kept us going full time. Celebrities we had our share too. Wilf Mannion the Middlesbrough and England inside left was a sanitary lance-corporal (a loo cleaner!) and Lieutenant Hedley Verity, the famous Yorkshire and England slow bowler (tragically killed later in Italy) were among my personal acquaintances. Wilf was a great man with blonde hair, big blue eyes and a terrific sense of humour - coupled with a really level temperament. The man that did so much for English football, now a labourer and in obscurity but oh how we could have done with him in the current World Cup!

Hedley Verity was a top class cricketer, and one of the original English gentlemen. In the summer evenings he would encourage net practice, and invite all and sundry to bowl at him. On one occasion I had the incredible luck to bowl him out. Actually I think the ball hit a spike holding down the mat and ricocheted through his legs - nevertheless I was cock-a-hoop for days after this.

Another pleasant interlude happened a few months later. All male soldiers were banished (less the band and a few pioneers) and the whole Depot turned into a ATS Training Centre (ATS being the forerunners of the WRAC). Drafts of beautiful blondes and stunning redheads - not to mention demure brunettes - floated around us like leaves in autumn. But after many mass invasions of love-hungry 'swaddies' from Catterick, and the resultant chaos, the scheme was abandoned. Pity! Pale, pimply recruits returned and it was 'as you were' much to our disgust. I was again feeling fidgety.

With all the action taking place on the world's war fronts, I felt I could do with a little myself. Every time Commandos or Paratroopers advertised in ACIs for volunteers I would rush to the Orderly Room but only to be baulked by Chippy.

However, my chance came at last. In early 1942 a directive was issued by the War Office stating that all bands would be trimmed to thirty two members (we were then forty one in strength) and to my great joy I found myself amongst the kick-outs!

But my elation was short-lived. There was to be no quick route to glory. We (the throw-outs) gleefully packed our kits and moved from the relative comfort of the band huts to the austere barrack rooms of 5 Infantry Training Centre, Gallowgate Camp - just four hundred yards from the Depot, but an entirely different world. We were each allocated to join a recruit squad, and it was no wonder that with our experience we were nearly all top recruits. Drill, discipline, weapons and sport were by this time second nature to us. At the end of six weeks we received our postings. I had hoped to be able to join our 1st battalion somewhere in the Middle East. But instead I was earmarked for the 10th (ERY) Green Howards. Originally Territorial Cavalry Regiment (East Riding Yeomanry), it was changed to an Infantry battalion on embodiment at the outbreak of war. My disappointment however was largely mollified by the fact that they were stationed at Dartford, Kent - just a few miles from my home and also that four ex-band comrades, George Bland (one of my enlistment chums), Reg Comley, 'Willy' Wilcox and Bill Hill (later killed by a sniper's bullet in Italy) were with me.

So after a short leave I found myself under canvas again in a field at Sutton-at-Hone, just outside Dartford, and as a member of 11 D-Day Platoon D Company, the 10th Green Howards.

Chapter 4
FROM HERE TO THERE - AND BACK!

Any ideas of a cushy holiday at home were soon to be nipped in the bud. Barely three days after our arrival, the Battalion marched out on a ten day exercise, moving through Kent and down towards the Sussex coast. Every night we slept in ditches or beneath trees but being high summer, we suffered no harm. All told, we covered 250 miles - an average of 25 miles a day. One rainy day the ration truck broke down and we went hungry. That happened to be the day we marched 34 miles!

The exercise was chiefly for the benefit of three Canadian Div. who later were known to gain glory by their courageous attack on Dieppe (also known as 'Exercise Jubilee') where casualties were high, but many lessons were learnt, which later saved countless lives on the next continental expedition - D-Day.

We staggered back to Sutton-at-Hone at last and our tents seemed like luxury hotels. On the first day back we were given three days leave and George Bland and I permitted ourselves the luxury of steak, egg and chips in a Dartford cafe, followed by a trip to the barbers for a shave - the one and only time in my life that I ever did this. I think it was a well merited reward. Our days at Dartford were numbered. We took the road for the Kent coast - Hythe to be exact, forming a part of the Division guarding the invasion-prone south coast. I cannot remember the name of our Division or even the number, but I can vividly remember our shoulder flashes - green squares with a red stripe across the base.

Hythe was a ghostly shadow of a pre-war holiday resort. The town was empty except for the troops, and thick barbed wire interspersed by machine gun and AA posts adorned the promenade. Our platoon was quartered in the thatched club house on the golf course, and it must have been absolute agony for the golfers in our midst to see the beautiful greens being used for weapon training and section tactics, with large ammunition boots churning up the grass. The beach was heavily mined, but I didn't really believe this until one day I saw a stray dog ease through the wire and onto the sands. Next second there was a deafening explosion and bits of dog flew in every direction. This effectively dampened any inclination for a swim on my part.

One unpleasant incident occurred about this time. I was sent on detached duty to nearby Lydd with a Canadian Infantry Regiment. One lunchtime I was alone in the barrack room lounging on my bed when four Focke Wulf hit-and-run raiders roared low over the square, dropping bombs and random and spraying the buildings with their guns. Our hut was extremely lucky. Although a neat row of holes ran the length of the building, nothing was damaged except for a few broken windows. The bombs however did more harm. Five huge craters appeared on the square, the cook-house was badly damaged and the medical and dental centre only fifty yards away, completely demolished. As the raiders passed over, so the air raid alert sounded!

I was pleased to learn that due to the alertness of the RAF, only two of the raiders managed to reach the French coast, but we worked until nightfall digging out the dead and injured from the M&D centre. All told, five were killed and a score injured, some very badly. It was one of a hundred such raids, but too near me for comfort. It was my first experience of low-level strafing and bombing (although I had some experience of the blitz) but it certainly wasn't to be the last.

After a few weeks I managed to get a brief leave, and while staying with my sister in Welling, Kent, received a telegram ordering me to report back to Otley in Yorkshire. Apparently the Battalion had moved again without telling me. Resignedly I proceeded north and found myself on 'Ilkla Moor Baht 'at'. My impression of Otley was in a minor key. It rained almost every minute of the short time that we were there, and the field in which our tents were pitched was nothing better than a swamp. Very little recreational facilities were available, and the local pubs were hotbeds of hostility - so most nights we either sat in our sopping tents and tried to read by candlelight, or bussed into Bradford to the dubious fleshpots there. On one unfortunate night I missed the last bus from Bradford, and had to leg it all the way back to camp. I arrived at 0330 hrs after a 12 mile walk. At 0730 hrs we were off again on a 15 mile route march! I slept well the following night.

It was at Otley that I volunteered to become a batman. Unfortunately my boss (a called up Lieutenant) was in civil life an inspector in the Flying Squad. I didn't know this then, but in no time at all he caught me filching his cigarettes and this, coupled with cold tea and cold shaving water at reveille, soon cut short my new-found career. Once again I found myself back in the platoon as a rifleman!

Having experienced very little Yorkshire hospitality in Otley (in spite of being a Yorkshire Regiment), most of us were sceptical about our next station which was to be Cottingham near Hull in East Yorkshire (our birthplace!). Perhaps this had some bearing on later attitudes but we thoroughly enjoyed our stay there.

The Battalion was widely dispersed with HQ in Cottingham, and the rifle companies spread out over the surrounding area. Military training slackened somewhat, and it was almost like a holiday. It was then that a Battalion concert party was formed, with two ex-professional comedians, Lieutenant Peter Cattle and Sgt Major Claude Harcourt (later killed by a shell from one of our own ships at Normandy) as the nucleus. All available talent was scraped together and then the brilliant idea of a supporting dance band came along. Volunteers were called for, and I jumped at this chance for a break from footslogging. Although only a mediocre oboe player, I took up the alto saxophone (same fingering, but different mouthpiece) with enthusiasm, and within a short space of time was making reasonable noises. The leader of our band, Cpl Milburn, was an ex-Radio Luxembourg pianist and accordionist, and was a brilliant musician. He was a long gangling character with a receding chin, sparse ginger hair and a real 'Geordie' accent. He hailed for the mining town of Ashington in Northumberland where he had been a miner, strangely enough being first cousin to the famous Jackie Milburn ('War Jackie'), the dynamic centre-forward of Newcastle United, and also related by marriage to the famous Charlton brothers, Bobby and Jacky of later fame. As a footballer however, none of the family talent touched him, but at the piano and behind the accordion he was unsurpassable. 'Ginger' Milburn is one of the characters that I will never forget. Other members of the band were Jackie Wood from Keighley - my great friend, and a good guitarist-cum-swing violinist. Sgt 'Maxie' Matthews on trumpet (a former 2nd Green Howards bandsman), Sgt 'Tich' Waite from Leeds on bass, Bill Hill (a fellow reject) on trombone, and last but not least, Art Walton, drums and vocals, ex-Teddy Joyce band and a true 'pro'.

Although not in the Heath or Miller mould, we nevertheless went over well and managed to get a regular Friday night spot in the magnificent Palais de Dance at nearby Withernsea. We also backed the Concert Party and contrived to do a few on-the-side jobs in local pubs.

Life was enjoyable in wartime Hull, but like all good things it soon came to an end. In November 1942, we paraded in full marching order (plus greatcoats) and took a slow troop train to the far south-west. After a grinding, cold journey we eventually arrived in Truro, Cornwall, in drizzling rain.

I was still in D Company, and we found ourselves in reasonable billets (shared by the mortar platoon) at Perranarworthal, midway between Truro and Falmouth. The Battalion was scattered over the mid-Cornwall area with HQ Company at Treliske Camp just outside Truro.

Now began serious Infantry training under our new CO Lt-Col. Parker. We spent a happy drunken Christmas and the Concert Party (with band) was much in demand. But in the New Year we sobered up and resumed training at an increased tempo. Route marches, field firing and night exercises lessened our fatness and increased our fitness. As winter turned into spring we steadily became the most proficient Infantry unit in the Division.

At this time, the 6th Airborne Division was in the process of formation. Infantry Regiments representing counties were being absorbed completely, thus it was no surprise to us that, as the premiere Battalion of the Division, we were selected to join 6 Airborne Division as a parachute regiment. For me, this was it!

Chapter 5
FITTENING UP

Around Easter 1943, the 10th Green Howards paraded at Treliske Camp for the last time. We formed a hollow square and Colonel Parker addressed the Battalion.

"Today we have been singled out as a unit with great potentiality" he roared.

"In fact, with so much potentiality, that we have been chosen to represent the county as a parachute battalion in the formation of the new 6th Airborne Division".

He paused.

"This is not a question of conscription and every man must be a willing volunteer. I therefore ask every Officer, NCO and man to step forward if he wishes to become a part of this great new adventure".

Ninety percent of the Battalion stepped forward.

With a few days leave tucked under out belts, we reported back to Hardwick Hall near Chesterfield (the town with the twisted church spire) for our initial parachute training. The remaining ten percent of the Battalion had been transferred to different Infantry Regiments and we lost sight of many old friends. But we could not find it in our hearts to condemn them for not volunteering. Paratrooping was not for everyone. In fact, most of them stormed the beaches of Normandy on D-Day, many to die (I met one or two of the survivors later for a drunken reunion). We were not reinforced, as the establishment of a para battalion was slightly less than that of an Infantry battalion. Before acceptance for parachute training, we were all thoroughly medically and dentally examined. Any history of a broken bone would mean instant rejection.

I think this was probably the most meticulous medical examination of our lives, but I could see the sense in it. An unfit soldier could be a liability or even a danger to his comrades in battle conditions.

Late April 1943 saw the start of our training. Hardwick Hall was a stately home, but we were quartered in nissen huts nearby. This was the 'get fit' stage of training and every day we paraded and ran for miles in full marching order. Discipline was strict, and no smoking was allowed outside the huts between reveille and retreat. Neither was walking - everyone doubled everywhere during the day! Physical training was predominant and strictly enforced. We just never stood still.

I think the most unpopular pastime was the battle course. It consisted of a series of severe obstacles, such as crawling through two feet diameter pipes, up nets and down again, across rope bridges over water, up and over twelve foot brick walls, across open ground (crawling) with live Bren gun fire six inches above our helmets, in full battle order. Nothing as exacting as this had happened to us as Infantrymen, consequently a few doubts were beginning to set in and a handful of the not-so-keen opted out.

The second half of the course was devoted to 'Synthetic Training' - that is the simulation of dropping through a hole in an aircraft. Mock apertures were set up consisting of a wooden platform twelve feet above the ground through which one dropped rigidly at attention onto a coir mat, hitting the ground with feet close together and smoothly taking the shock by falling sideways. This attention position was not the ravings of a drill maniac, but the sensible way of leaving a plane/balloon. The head, being the heaviest part of the body, must be kept absolutely upright otherwise it would unbalance the whole body striking the head on the side of the aperture, commonly known as 'ringing the bell'.

Inevitably several casualties overtook us. One Company Sgt Major was unlucky enough to break an arm during a mock drop, and the occupant of the bunk above me (we slept in massive wooden bunks with the top on six feet above the concrete floor), dreaming of the future no doubt, leapt out of bed during the night and, crashing to the floor, broke both ankles.

These, and several other fracture cases, were instantly RTU'd (Returned To Unit, but in this case posted to an Infantry Regiment). Sprains, cuts and bruises were commonplace. I estimate we lost 5% of our strength at Hardwick.

We moved to Ringway in June 1943. All of us keen (but just a little teeny bit scared!) to get on with the next stage.

Ringway Airport, just outside of Manchester, was a pre-war civil airport. It was taken over by the RAF early in the war for the specific purpose of advanced parachute synthetic training and actual dropping. Three barrage balloon (each nicknamed Bessie) and five tired old Whitley bombers converted to para dropping were available. The inevitable nissen huts were there, and of course the runways. Although the planes took off from Ringway, the actual drop was made at nearby Tatton Park, as were the balloon jumps. An additional feature in the park was a large lake - which had claimed several victims. I heard a story about a Polish soldier who had been on a previous course. It appears that he was afraid to jump (from the plane) and his indignant comrades kicked him to the rear where he lay squirming with shame. Suddenly he hurled himself down the aperture and, without a second's hesitation, dived out. Unfortunately for him he had forgotten to hitch up his static line and he plummeted straight into Tatton Park lake. They never found his body.

This and other wild stories circulated freely. But we tried to ignore them as we settled in for the final stage. Large hangers lined the runway at Ringway and to these palaces of thrills (or torture) each morning we were marched. The training aids were varied and some were masterpieces in substitution for the real thing. We climbed to the roof of one hanger and, holding grimly onto a handle with a pulley in the centre, slung it over a rope and descended rapidly from fifty feet up to ground level, there to make a 'feet together' landing on two coir mats (if we were lucky!).

These training devices ranged from swinging through space in a parachute harness and jumping from a real fuselage (without a chute) to the 'fan'. The fan was a diabolical piece of engineering which necessitated sitting above an aperture in a wooden platform and clad in a parachute harness, plunging through the hole towards the ground sixty feet below. The static line connected to the harness would activate a fan, progressively slowing the rate of descent until the trainee reached the mats and would be hitting the deck as if on an actual drop. This theory didn't always work!

The week after we left Ringway, our former instructor, a Flight Sgt Baker RAF was killed when the fan slipped and failed to slow his descent, plunging him to his death from the platform. The authorities then decided that this form of training was too dangerous and scrapped it. We could have told them this weeks earlier. I think all of us had suffered a bruise, scrape, cut or sprain from this wretched device at sometime or another.

The classroom was not neglected. We were given lectures and demonstrations on the composition, capabilities and quality of the parachute (no doubt to give us a little confidence) and we visited the parachute packing sheds where WAAF girls packed them with meticulous care on long tables. It was indeed a specialised occupation, the girls receiving 3d per day extra duty pay for this highly responsible task. Not one of us attempted a romantic liaison with them (the girls, not the parachutes!). The possible results of a lovers' quarrel would be too awful to contemplate! So we just sheepishly grinned and moved on.

Later we were taught to pack our own - sometimes with dire results.

Chapter 6
THE BIG DROP

Suddenly we were ready for our first jump. On a fine summer's evening in July 1943 we embussed for Tatton Park wearing our rubber helmets - adorned with chalked slogans such as 'S- or bust', 'We're coming Adolph', 'Boro for the cup' etc, drew our parachutes, signed the logbook (each chute had it's own logbook, and after fifty drops was 'pensioned off') and then paraded in three ranks by each 'Bessie'. After watching the monster go up and down several times it was at last my turn. With a dry mouth through fear and over-smoking, and vainly trying to suppress the countless butterflies in my stomach, I lurched towards the plywood cage in company with three other cowards. A brief check of harness and release plate, and then into Bessie's undercarriage.

We sat one in each corner holding grimly onto an iron handle, with our static lines clipped to a central overhead bar and with the great circular hole below us. At the given signal bawled by the dispatcher,

"Six hundred feet with four dropping", we went.

The winch made noises and the contraption lurched upwards towards the steely evening sky. The jovial banter of the instructor lessened in humour as the plywood contraption floated higher, until eventually we jerked to a stop, swaying a little in the evening breeze. The view from that height was superb. In the distance, the great city of Manchester lay sprawling in the evening sun with a slight smoke haze over the industrial suburbs. Directly below us, the fields appeared on as big as postage stamps, with Tatton Park lake looking more like a puddle than an acre of water. But there was little time to admire the scenery.

"Action stations number one!"

The poor devil swung his legs over the edge of the hole, his face set in a frozen mask of fear.

"Go!"

There was a slight scuffle, a violent lurch of the cage, and we were one less. I daren't look at number two as he went out in the same manner. Strangely enough it wasn't the drop that really worried me, it was the awful possibility of the cable snapping and Bessie (with us hanging below) drifting off into the skies of Lancashire like a latter-day Flying Dutchman - never to descend.

Then it was my turn.

I can scarcely recall going through that hole, but it felt like falling down the lift shaft of the Empire State Building. Earth and sky dissolved into a mad whirl of green, brown and blue. My recall to sanity was a savage jerk as the canopy developed and I swung underneath it. Then it became a dreamlike drift towards Mother Earth. Completely forgetting my training, I was forcibly reminded by a great amplified voice from below.

"Get your bloody feet together number three!"

I hastily complied, and then the grass of Tatton Park rushed up to meet me. I arrived with a rather heavy bump, but all the hard training helped me to absorb the shock. I rolled over, jumped to my feet and collapsed the 'chute. Rolling it up, I dropped the whole bundle onto a nearby three-tonner (for some unfortunate girl to repack at 3d per day!) then swaggered over to the YMCA canteen (yes, a nissen hut) on the edge of the park (on a later jump, one of our mortar platoon was to land on the roof). At this moment and cuppa and a cigarette (sold singly at 1d) with a sympathetic smile from a dear old WVS lady was all I wanted in life. As a compatriot remarked, "Terra Firma - the more firmer, the less terror!"

At this point, a word or two must be said about the instructors. All sergeants and flight sergeants (and, of course, volunteers) performed the hazardous task of training thousands of troops continuously. There was a good chance of injury or even death in their occupation, but with their sympathy, cheerfulness and dedication they gave us all the greatest confidence. On this, our first drop, the sergeant, after despatching us all safely, lightly vaulted over the side of the basket and landed upright - technically known as a 'stand up' landing. This was his 253rd jump.

Flushed with pride (and a certain amount of relief), we tackled number two balloon. It was a dull, overcast morning and due to the atmospheric conditions we went slightly higher - to 800 feet - but the sensation was identical. This time I remembered the training, and the amplifier was quiet. I made a good landing, which gave me a little more confidence. I needed this for the third balloon drop - the dreaded night drop.

At two o'clock in the morning we were elevated into a moonless sky. It was so dark, I could barely see the others. Then at 700 feet we plunged into the inky blackness with no idea of when the ground would arrive. It did come, however, with a great thump, but luckily no injury. One of our Junior Officers was not quite so lucky, and broke his back - thus ending his parachute career.

Three balloons had now been accomplished and it was time for the aircraft. We paraded and emplaned in an ancient Whitley bomber. Ten of us (known as a 'stick') squeezed into the narrow fuselage - it was extremely cramped. Five sat forward of the aperture and five astern facing each other alternately. Above the aperture were two lights - one red, one green. When the red light came on, one of the pair by the aperture would swing his legs over and into space, at the same time watching the lights. On the green light glowing, he would thrust himself outwards and drop. The opposite man would drop immediately afterwards. On this occasion we dropped in 'slow pairs' i.e. two only at a time, as the old Whitley lumbered around Tatton Park.

The sensation on exiting, however, was completely different. The slipstream impact was like hitting a brick wall, and the parachute opened almost immediately. It could be most frightening to be above a deployed canopy, and suddenly drop to below it. But on the whole, I found it to be a lot better than the 'lift shaft' sensation of the balloon - things happened quicker! The real danger was to become entangled in the rigging lines and come down head first. Unfortunately, some did.

Following the 'slow pairs' came the 'slow half stick' i.e. five out on each circuit. Then the whole stick, all moving out as swiftly as possible, as every second's delay in the plane could mean a gap of hundreds of yards on the ground. The whole object was to hit as low as possible and to assemble on the DZ as closely together as conditions would allow. Containers with rifles and equipment were also dropped (halfway through each stick) and, on reaching the ground, it was imperative to grab weapons quickly and form up in a circular defensive pattern before linking up with other sticks. This was the theory, but in practice it rarely happened. I recall in one training jump months later, a member of my stick 'jibbed' i.e. refused to jump and blocked the exit. Unfortunately, I was the last of the stick and, after a heated argument, I finally had to almost dive over him and through the hole (I didn't fancy a Court Martial) with the subsequent result that I was miles behind the rest of the stick and, instead of landing on a nice clear area of grassland, I smashed through the top branches of several trees on the edge of a wood and made a bad landing. Needless to say I took very little part in that exercise!

By now we had completed six of our eight jumps. The next two were drops involving the whole Battalion and using over fifty aircraft (borrowed from Bomber Command). On the very last one we did a brief exercise simulating the capture of a German gun position. This was a bad one for me as I landed rather heavily on my right foot and it ached for days.

We were now fully qualified parachutists and received our wings from the RAF Group Captain in the Garrison Cinema. The poor man had to shake over five hundred hands and reply to over five hundred salutes that day, so I should imagine his gin and tonic glass must have trembled a little that night! After the ceremony we dispersed on leave for seventeen glorious days with great glee and a glorious end of term feeling.

Most of us sewed our wings on in the train!

Chapter 7
LARKS IN LARKHILL

After a return from our respective fleshpots and comfortably sated with beer, women and song, we surveyed Larkhill with a dismal eye.

It was set right in the middle of Salisbury Plain which, at that time, was seething with feverish military activity from Andover in the east, to Salisbury in the south. Everywhere were camps, vehicles and marching troops. All nations and nearly all arms were represented from Americans and Canadians to Free French and Poles. Nearby were the immaculate lines of the Glider Pilot Regiment, and their small Austers were constantly practicing landings and take offs on any available stretch of grass. We occupied a camp divided by a large barrack square, one side being occupied by ourselves and the other side by the 13th (Lancashire) Battalion. That sounds like the weigh-in to a big fight - on occasions it was just that.

The accommodation, consisting of large wooden barrack huts set out in 'spider' formation, was clean and warm. Amesbury, the nearest bit of civilisation, was a bus ride away. To travel on the last bus from there back to Larkhill was quite an experience - drunken singing, vomiting and outbreaks of violence were commonplace. Blue language filled the air regardless of any females aboard (there were very few). I really felt sorry for the poor bus crew, having to endure this nightly, but Sunday School behaviour could not have been expected and a large percentage of these passengers were unknowingly in the last few months of their lives. Salisbury was much further away, but still accessible. From my barrack room bedside window, Stonehenge was a mere three hundred yards away, with the Plain stretching away behind it to the south.

We were now officially known as the 12th (Yorkshire) Battalion of the Parachute Regiment. We wore the famous 'Pegasus' Divisional sign, 'airborne' below it and with the pale blue lanyard - denoting the Battalion colours - completing the body trappings. We changed cap badges from our old Green Howards ones to the Army Air Corps (an eagle set in a laurel wreath) and later to the new Parachute Regiment - a pair of wings centred by a parachute and surmounted by the crown and lion.

The 12th, 13th and 7th (Essex) Parachute Battalions constituted the newly formed 5th Para Brigade, commanded by Brigadier Nigel Poett. The Divisional Commander was Major General 'Windy' Gale, a courageous and kindly soldier who completely belied his nickname. The Battalion, under Lt Col Parker, was composed of 75% ex-Green Howards, but they slowly wasted out until D-Day, when I estimate it was down to 45%.

Training restarted. In the new role we were expected to drop behind enemy lines and capture strategic objectives, fighting independently until relieved by ground forces. In fact we were not Infantry dropped from the air, but (modestly I say this) Super Infantry!

On the social side, the concert party re-emerged under their new title of 'Happy Landings' and continued a successful career. Most of the tunes were with us still, some as 'jumpers' and the rest as ground staff. The dance band under Ginger Milburn (now NCO in charge of the dining hall) was in the same position. We played at the weekly dance in the gymnasium which separated the 12th and 13th Battalions. Strangely enough, although these were drunken affairs suffering from a chronic lack of women, I saw very little violence.

In fact, there was a great deal of fun. On one occasion during the interval, Jacky Wood stuffed a doughnut up the bell of Maxie Matthew's trumpet. Maxie had been getting a little pompous of late and we decided to teach him a lesson. After the interval, we started up with 'That's A'Plenty' and there was a noticeable lack of sound from the trumpet. Maxie's face went from red to blue to purple and suddenly a mangled jam doughnut shot halfway across the floor to the accompaniment of a hideous blurb of sound. The crowd was convulsed but Maxie was furious and he never spoke to any of us for days!

On our extra parachute pay (2/6d a day), we spent many hilarious and drunken weekends in 'the Smoke', staying at the TOC H in Westminster and being strenuously ejected in turn from such entertainment centres as the Hammersmith Palais, Streatham Locarno and Covent Garden (then a huge ballroom with two bands). We really loved these rollicking breaks from the rigours of training.

However, all was not fun and games. The build up to a 'second front' was slowly grinding into gear and training was taking on a more urgent note. To my utter surprise, I found myself posted to HQ Company - Intelligence Section. This selection in no way indicated a superior intellectual capacity, merely another mundane Battalion task - like the MT, the Mortar Platoon, Cooks, Signals etc. But to me it was infinitely better than a rifle company. Our little group consisted of the Intelligence Officer and Sergeant plus twelve other ranks. The function of the section was to make maps (from aerial photographs), build sand models from briefings and provide disposition reports for the CO. In addition we learnt the uniforms and ranks of the Wehrmacht, the recognition of enemy aircraft and vehicles, and a little German (Hände hoch! Marsch-marsch! etc).

Parachuting was not forgotten by a long way. Once a month we did a balloon drop at nearby Bulford and the occasional plane drop when they were available.

It was there than I saw my first parachute accident. The unfortunate victim was a young nineteen year old from B Company named Wilson. On the preceding day he had 'jibbed' from an aircraft and, in accordance with the current regulations, was put under close arrest to await Court Martial. The refusal was an automatic sentence of eighty four days detention. I believed that he had some domestic problems on his mind which were worrying him and, in light of this, authority (in the shape of the Adjutant), relented and gave him one more chance.

We were seated on the grass with parachutes strapped on, smoking the usual last minute 'nerves' cigarette. Two balloons were operating and all seemed normal when suddenly there were shouts and, to my horror, I saw a body hurtling to the ground in a candle[1]. With a sickening thud, he hit the ground and bounced once. By the time we reached him, he was dead and in a shocking mess. We watched dumbly as the 'Blood Wagon' bounced across the field to pick him up. Dropping was then cancelled for the day - the official reason given was that hostile aircraft were in the vicinity, but I think it was more connected with our morale. Poor Wilson was the first death in the Battalion and the only one in training. He was given a military funeral in his home town in Yorkshire.

Another bad accident took place a little later. A 'Sprog' pilot reading his altimeter incorrectly, dropped a stick from 150 feet. Although there were no deaths, five of the stick, including a Major, were crippled for life.

---

[1] A 'Roman Candle' i.e. a parachute which does not develop. The speed of descent causes high friction, thus setting the underdeveloped canopy alight.

Chapter 8
MAINLY PLANES AND NAVIGATION

Aircraft were naturally at a premium at that time and it was always a continual battle with RAF Bomber Command to borrow even ageing Whitleys for training purposes. Halifaxes and Stirlings were tried and, although the Stirling proved a success, not so the Halifax. We did one trial jump from this aircraft, but it was a dismal (and could have been a dangerous) failure. Its slowest speed without stalling was about 120mph - compared with 85mph of a Whitley. Inside it was like sitting in a cathedral after the cramped confines of a Whitley and, although it was a floor drop, the aperture seemed to go down forever. Our exit was nearly lethal and spread us over half of Wiltshire. The Halifax was 'sacked' as a paratroop vehicle, although it continued as a bomber for quite a time.

The Short Stirling was far better. Rough platforms ran the length of the fuselage on both sides and this was an improvement on floor crouching. It was also a 'door exit' which meant that, after hooking up to the overhead rail, one simply walked out at the tail! This was quite a novelty (although the Germans and Americans had been using this technique for ages). Instead of containers, we carried kit bags anchored to the legs, making it a much faster exit. The Armstrong Whitworth Albemarle came into use at about this time and was later used extensively in action. The stick sat on a shelf within the fuselage. The narrow aft end of the plane contained a long aperture measuring roughly eight feet by three feet and covered by tissue paper. We hooked up to an overhead rail and, on the green light, sat behind each other 'bunny hopping' into space with the first man breaking the paper. This was a very difficult way to exit from an aircraft and would have been rather uncomfortable in action, so thankfully that was the one and only Albemarle jump for me. Although they were used by the 9th Battalion on D-Day.

We did two jumps from a C10 Douglas Dakota and these were good ones as the 'Dak' was a steady plane which could slow down to a 'jumpable' speed. They were one of the most versatile aircraft of the war and were used for almost everything in the transport field. As a tribute to this fine aircraft, one has been preserved and now sits outside the Airborne Forces Museum in Aldershot.

By this time I had done twenty jumps and was beginning to feel like a veteran. One hot summer's day we emplaned for a training exercise and, aboard three Whitleys, took off for Hurn Airport to make the DZ at Durrington to the north. By some amazing chance, although flying in line astern, we found ourselves over the coast of France! It was scheduled to be a twenty minute flight but took us over three hours. The temperature inside the aircraft was like an oven - no insulation or air conditioning, just the sun heating the aluminium fuselage like a frying pan. Over the French Coast we were fired at by hostile Ack Ack Batteries, but it must have been an off day for them as nothing hit us. Eventually out bewildered leading navigator picked up the route to Durrington, but it was too late. The soldier sitting opposite me, who had eaten far too much for lunch, suddenly went red, white and green before vomiting all over my legs, filling his 'sick' bag and continuing to fill everybody else's! The stench was awful and the air blue. I blessed Providence for a strong stomach. By now we were circling the DZ, but the sick man lay back and absolutely refused to jump. I had to climb out over him to jump - no mean feat dressed as we were (this was the jump that I mentioned in Chapter 6). I learned afterwards that the pilot had called him up to the flight deck after we had all jumped, but there he had distinguished himself even further by vomiting all over the controls! Appropriately enough, his name was Frank Tuck!

Another navigational error had more agreeable results. It was normal training to take a section out in a closed truck in the dark and drop them off by pairs to find their way back to barracks, usually involving a cross-country march of about ten miles. This was a very necessary part of training, as we were to find out later.

One evening at about dusk, we did this trip and I found myself together with a jovial East Anglian character named Barrett (or was it Barnet?) stranded in the middle of nowhere listening to the sound of the truck's engine dying away in the distance. Barrett was a confident and self-acclaimed expert of the map and compass but it was no surprise to me that an hour later, after splashing through streams, trudging over ploughed fields and blundering through pitch-black wood, he begrudgingly admitted that we were completely and absolutely lost. I was furious - I'd wanted to get back before the NAAFI beer bar closed and here we were in the middle of nowhere with not a pint in sight.

I told Barrett a few home truths as we sulked our way down a muddy lane. Suddenly, in front of us were the lights of a pub. We started to live again! Joyfully we shrugged rifle and equipment off and entered. Inside, the smokey, warm atmosphere was like Heaven to us. Barrett, the farmer, was at home immediately with these Wiltshire farm hands and, within minutes, free beer was flowing like a river into our very receptive mouths. The piano started up and we bawled forth agreeable renderings of disagreeable parachute songs. The locals replied with bawdy versions of their own and the evening ended in a glorious pink haze of conviviality - then we were out on the road again.

Fortunately for us, I'd found out our exact position and didn't need a map - I couldn't have seen it anyway. We were only a few miles from Larkhill and, being the more sober (?) of the duo, I steered a singing drunken East Anglian along the dark country roads, arriving in barracks at around three in the morning.

Unfortunately we had an RSM's drill parade at 0900 hours!

Chapter 9
THE RUN IN

This then was our training. We did long forced route marches, weapon training, drill, sport and exercise involving the attack and destruction of a German gun emplacement. This, of course, was the Merville Battery - which later was allocated to the 9th Battalion. I was fortunate enough to be sent on a Foreign Weapons Course at nearby Bulford and had an intensely interesting week firing and studying German Spandeau, the Italian Beretta Family (of revolvers!) and Russian anti-tank rifles.

On one exercise, the Intelligence Platoon were provided with little folding motorcycles! Although they were great fun, they were of limited practical value and we never saw them again. Folding cycles were also used, but these passed the test and were used extensively by the Airborne Division later.

Periods of leave were sparse, but we still managed the odd thirty six hour weekend in London. However it was becoming evident that D-Day was approaching rapidly. Occasionally we would see a piece of 'top brass' with the CO in close attendance, strolling round the camp, watching the training and assessing the morale of the Battalion. A slight tenseness, or perhaps an awareness, was building up. Rumours circulated wildly and the most fantastic stories were believed - even the one that we were to drop on Berlin, assassinate Hitler and short-circuit the whole war!

In early May we assembled in the vast gymnasium (doors closely guarded by MPs) to receive the general briefing, under conditions of strict security. Four of us had made the huge sand model of part of Normandy and, with justifiable pride, watched the CO point out our task on it.

It transpired that the 6th Airborne Division had been allocated two primary tasks for D-Day. Firstly, the bridges over the Caen Canal and the River Orme (running roughly parallel) were to be captured intact and held to enable seaborne Infantry and Armour penetration of North Normandy and the Caen Plain. Secondly, the destruction of the Merville Battery, which would be a vicious thorn in the flesh of any disembarking armies on the Normandy beaches. We also leaned that the 9th Battalion, under Lt Col Otway, would be responsible for this formidable task as the Merville Battery was said to be almost impregnable. For this let-off we heaved silent sighs of relief, but nevertheless trooped out of the gymnasium in a subdued mood.

A few days later we paraded in best battledress at Bulford and were there inspected by HM King George VI, HRH The Queen and HRH Princess Elizabeth (then eighteen years old). The King looked thin and frail, but his eyes glowed with pride as thousands of voices cheered him at the end of the parade. It was my second meeting with him. Two years earlier I had been recalled from leave to beat cymbals in the Green Howards band on Richmond Barracks Square when Their Majesties had inspected the Depot.

It seemed more like fifty years.

In late May 1944 the Battalion left Larkhill and embussed for our transit camp at Netheravon, not very far away. Security here was really tight. The tented camp close to the airship was encompassed by double rolls of barbed wire and continuously lit by powerful lights. CMPs and dog handlers prowled by day and night. To get in and out was practically impossible - we really felt like prisoners of war. All mail of course was strictly censored, but being a lethargic letter writer, it didn't really matter to me.

We now really seemed to be in another world. The Battalion turned inwards on itself. We sunbathed, played a little football, drank a considerable amount of beer and smoked like chimneys. Cards and tombola (an ancestor of bingo) were also extremely popular during this period of inactivity.

The Padre was always drifting around the Companies dispensing a little Heavenly inspiration wherever needed. A huge six foot four ex-Oxford rugger blue, it was confidently expected that on his exit from the 'plane he would go upwards! He didn't however (well, not on D-Day), but his calm confidence warmed us all and he was one of the finest 'God-botherers' that I had the privilege to meet.

Our Quartermaster, a jovial red-faced Yorkshireman, did us proud. From his Aladdin's Cave he produced hitherto unheard of delicacies in the food line, wonderful films projected in the NAAFI tent (sometimes upside down, to our great delight!) and of course everything in the clothing line - including an unlimited supply of the famous grey-back socks. I believe he came through unscratched and now runs a little tobacconists in the wilds of Halifax.

The Medical Officer, a dour Scot, was not in great demand, especially for constipation, but he and his little ream of RAMC and Regimental Medics were merely resting before the storm. Sadly he was killed later in a mortar attack at Ranville.

Everything possible had been done, we were trained, kitted and mentally prepared for any eventuality 'over there'. *Alea iacta est*- the die is cast!

The trumpets sounded on June 5th 1944. In the morning we paraded, were issued with French Francs, made out our wills (I had precious little to leave to anyone) and sat down to wait.

At 1400 hours we paraded, kitted in full battle order, consisted of a scrimmed-up helmet, web equipment, fifty rounds of .303, six 2" mortar bombs, compass, revolver (which I was hopelessly inadequate in using), map case, pencils - right down to a pack of toilet paper (affectionately known as 'Army Form Blank') plus, of course, a 24 hour K Ration. We then stood down until 1800.

As we queued up to partake in our last English meal, we could see the Stirlings parked near the runway, distinguished by their high flight cabins and huge single tail planes, all lit by the late afternoon sun. I looked around and wondered how many of this cheerful, noisy queue would be alive at this time tomorrow. My knees turned to jelly and now I knew for a fact something that I had suspected for a long time. I was a Mark I Coward! I'm afraid I couldn't eat much at this Last Supper.

We were issued with pills - ostensibly to ensure relaxation and sleep on the aircraft, but in actual fact, a drug against the terrors of the night. I put mine into the pocket of my smock and discovered them three weeks later. We fell in three ranks and received a thorough inspection by the Company Commander.

It was a lovely sunset as we marched out towards the dark aircraft. We clambered aboard and clumsily seated ourselves on the wooden benches as the pilots warmed up the engines. All conversation was effectively dampened by the roaring of hundreds of engines around us and, in the sickly light from the few weak bulbs in the roof, we looked like monsters from outer space. The roar continued for some time and then whined up to a crescendo and I realised we were moving down the runway fast. With a gentle lurch we were airborne.

Chapter 10
THE MOMENT OF REVELATION

The noise gradually decreased as the pilot reached his assigned altitude and throttled back the four engines. It began to get a little colder, although we couldn't have been all that high. The steady drone lulled us into a cat-nap, but it seemed as if we were in that cramped cell for hours - which may well have been the case. It was no direct flight from here to there, but a series of wide circles as the squadrons integrated into formation. Conversation didn't exactly flourish, although a little wit did try and get through.

Suddenly the plane rocked a little, and then more violently. Above the engine drone came dull crumping sounds. We didn't have to be told we were now crossing the coast of France and that this was our welcome. The pilot's evasion tactics continued for a short time and then ceased as we moved further inland. The order came to hook up and then the red light glowed like an evil eye. We scrambled into jump positions as the Sergeant stick commander struggled with the heavy door. We lined up, clutching kitbags, as the aircraft lurched wildly under intense anti-aircraft fire.

"This will be a good thing to get out of" I thought to myself.

The green light glowed and away we went.

At first it seemed like another night exercise as my 'chute opened swiftly. Then I saw tracer arching up slowly from the ground and knew this was the real thing. As I descended, the clatter of automatic weapons together with rifle fire became louder and pinpoint flashes with a few small fires could be seen. Around me was the vague outline of hundreds of canopies and the occasional faint scream as a swinging body was hit. Several died in the air and many more were wounded, including our former CO Colonel Parker, who had four fingers sliced off by an unlucky hit. So much for our strict security - the Germans knew we were coming and this was the welcome party. I was petrified as the automatic fire raked the skies at random, expecting at any second to be riddled. It seemed to be an eternity since leaving the plane.

Suddenly I saw a darker mass below me and, before I knew it, crashed through tree branches to end up swinging gently about six feet above the undergrowth. I twisted and banged the release box and dropped awkwardly onto France, right on my gammy foot. It was quite painful but could have been worse - I could have been turned into a sieve!

I crouched under a tree and tried to pull myself together. The night was alive with noise - the roar of hundreds of aircraft and the harsh rattle of small arms fire punctuated by the deeper crump of mortars. Now and then a bright light lit up the scene as a flare exploded in the sky. It seemed to me that I was on the edge of a wood or forest. In the light of one of these flares I saw a shadowy figure emerge from behind a tree.

I pointed my revolver at it and croaked.

> "Who's there?"

Not very military, but the reply was even less so.

> "Mind tha' own bloody business, where the f***ing hell is 'C' Company?"

> "No idea mate" I said.

> "Well, we'd better bloody look then!"

I had no inkling as to who my companion was, but we set off together in the direction of a flashing red lamp. That was the predetermined rallying signal and, sure enough, when we reached it we found a few dozen of the Battalion there, all in prone firing positions.

Spandeau fire - distinguishable by its rapid rate of 600 rounds per minute (our Brens fired only 450) - was raking the area, making it an extremely uncomfortable place to occupy. Some of us (not being the stuff heroes are made of) wormed our way backwards into a shallow hollow of ground and kept our heads down. Probably the enemy were using fixed lines of fire as the assault died down after a short time. We then seized this opportunity to retreat through a straggly hedgerow to a sunken country lane and attain our ground object - an old stone quarry.

Here we became a little more organised. Rifles and Brens were retrieved and distributed and we gradually turned into a fighting force. Confidence returned as we filled magazines and loaded weapons.

At first I was in mixed company but soon found the section - less the Sergeant and two others (Frank Tuck was one - he was badly wounded in the air). We never saw the remaining two again. Lt Jones the Intelligence Officer led us away from the firing to the company rendezvous, where we lay low in a cowshed for a short time. But there was little peace, the mortars of 21st Panzer Division plastered the area continuously and the swish and crump of shells from our ships off the coast were relentlessly dropping onto enemy positions - too near to be comfortable.

Glider troops were now landing in force and searchlights made the night as bright as day. Unfortunately one of our own shells landed on 'C' Company HQ, killing two officers and ten others - one of whom was our favourite comedian Sergeant Major Claude Harcourt. A pink glow in the sky heralded the dawn. We were now digging in south of Le Bas de Ranville on the edge of a wood. The open country to the south was ideal for tanks and it was from this direction it was expected that the 21st Panzer would mount its attack. We stood to after digging in and the 3rd and 4th anti-tank regiment, armed with 6 pounders and 17 pounders, moved into positions in line with us and just inside the wood. Hot tea, together with K Rations helped the morale a little and we continued excavating our slit trenches in a somewhat happier mood.

During the day we saw several units of German Infantry - probably Panzer Grenadiers and, although some firing ensued, there was no major attack.

Possibly they were a probing patrol testing for strength. Later a German SP (self-propelled) gun appeared and was promptly destroyed by the anti-tank boys. 'Charlie' Company repelled a sharp attack in the early afternoon with some losses, but fortunately no supporting armour appeared.

In the early evening the Intelligence Officer and myself were detailed to bring in two German prisoners for interrogation by Brigade HQ (Int). As we moved through C Company positions we saw signs of the afternoon's battle in which six were killed and fifteen wounded. The MO, together with his orderlies, were hard at work, patching up the wounded and evacuating the dead. At Company HQ we found a bored Corporal smoking with one hand and training a Sten gun on two prisoners, seated with hands on heads, with the other. I was quite surprised to find that these two Nazi Supermen were indeed very human. One was a blonde youth, the other an older grizzled type. Both appeared to be scared stiff and, on the command 'Hände hoch - marsch', leapt to their feet and preceded us through the woods as if eager to leap into captivity. The IO, being of a practical turn of mind, snarled at them.

"Halt - wo ist Ihre Armbanduhr?"
(Stop - where is your wristwatch?)

"Bitte, wir haben keine Armbanduhren."
(Please, we have no watches.)

At that moment I could imagine a certain Corporal in C Company admiring two Kraut watches - one on each wrist!

On the following day we were relieved by the 12th Devons, who had arrived by sea. They were twice our strength (in numbers) and took over our positions with great enthusiasm. It was really heartwarming to see these big farm boys in uniform arrive and we knew that without a doubt that they would give the Nazis a lot of trouble. We then packed up and moved back through the woods to Longueval to take up fresh positions, rather annoyed that we had dug the Devons' defences for them! At

Longueval we were mortared and shelled and lost fifty more of our depleted Battalion.

The Royal Ulster Rifles joined up with us and took defence of Longueval while we withdrew back to the relative safety of our reserve position along the Orme River in a disused quarry near the bridge. Nobody was very happy about this as we had taken the brunt of two initial attacks and were then withdrawn twice. In other words (Yorkshire dialect) 'we were being boogered abaht'.

However, we all admitted it was exceedingly pleasant to just dig in and get a good hot meal, a wash and a shave. Despite the continuous shelling, I got a good nights' sleep!

Chapter 11
ONWARDS, AIRBORNE SOLDIERS

We remained static for several days and life became almost normal. Mail and fresh rations arrived and morale began to rise by degrees. Not a lot of Intelligence work was required as we were on the sidelines of the battle. The Int. Corps boys in Division HQ knew who we were up against.

But there were other tasks to perform like unloading ammunition, roofing slit trenches, digging in strong points and wiring vulnerable sites. On rare occasions we were visited by the decreasing Luftwaffe, but mainly the RAF and USAAF controlled the skies. Gliders were still landing with troops and supplies, although by now the massive seaborne armies had established their beachhead and were steadily pushing inland. At this moment we only waited.

Further south however, all was not so rosy and desperate battles were being fought. The 857th Panzer Regiment used one of its Battalions to try and recapture the Orne River and the Caen Canal bridges, but they ran foul of Lovat's Commandoes (numbers 4 and 6) and were bloodily repulsed. Notwithstanding this setback, they tried again from the south and the south-east. This time the brunt of the attack was taken by the 7th and 13th Paras. It was amazing to note that the Germans advanced casually across open ground and were mown down like rabbits, but they still came. Reinforcements were obviously beginning to build up.

General Gale now decided to take the village of Bréville - very strongly held and of great strategic value as it overlooked Ranville and the Caen Plain - a real thorn in the side of the Divisional advance.

The first attempt was a lamentable failure. The 9th Battalion plus the 1st Black Watch supported by the Artillery of the 51st Highland Division, made a determined attempt from the south-west. But the enemy, with superior Infantry strength and hastily summoned self-propelled guns, asserted themselves and repulsed the attack. Casualties were high, especially with the Jocks. Heavy mortaring and the lethal MG34s forced the attackers to fall back. The 9th Battalion, depleted by their earlier destruction of the Merville Battery, were almost overrun and, even with the assistance of the big guns of HMS Arethusa, were no match for Rommel's men. The situation was rapidly deteriorating and 'Windy' had to think again.

He now decided to try from the north. 12th Battalion (now down to 8 officers and 350 ORs), together with D Company of the Devons, and backed by the Sherman tanks of the 13/18th Hussars and the artillery of 51 Division, would make the attempt.

On 12 June at approximately 1900 hrs, the CO, Lieutenant Colonel Johnson was called to Divisional HQ and there, with the other Commanding Officers, was personally briefed by General Gale. In short the plan was to make an attack at 2200 hrs that night whilst a diversion would be made from the south at the same time.

The start line was to be Amfreville and ourselves and the Devons, back by the tanks and artillery, would attack on a Company front with C landing followed by A, then B, then Devons and HQ Company.

There was a slight feeling of resentment about this, more as it appeared that we were the odd-job boys for the 6th Airlanding Brigade instead of being part of our own 5 Para Brigade, but we had little time for resentment of any kind as there was only an hour left.

We blackened faces, scrimmed up helmets, check and rechecked arms and ammunition and, with dry mouths, awaited events. The Intelligence section had now been spread across the Battalion and myself, together with Bill Harrison and a L/Cpl, were attached to B Company.

At exactly 2030 hrs we left the quarry and moved towards the start line, reaching it within 30 minutes. Quickly we moved into our positions and the tanks came up in the rear.

At 2150 hrs the artillery barrage commenced and the noise was unbelievable. Smoke and flames erupted in the village as the artillery pounded it, assisted by the guns of the Hussars' tanks. It was difficult to see how any living creature could survive such a bombardment, but they did! Mortars and shells from the German Panzers were dropping amongst us to prove that the defenders were still very much alive.

At 2200 hrs on the dot the noise stopped and C Company moved off. A Company joined them within minutes and my heart was pounding madly as it became our turn. In the twilight we could hear the pounding of mortars and the rattle of small arms fire punctuated by shouts and screams.

As we crouched in the hedgerow awaiting the summons, one of B Company 's Corporals (an old chum from Larkhill) shouted to me:

"Get your sax out Windy, that'll flatten 'em!"

I managed to produce a sickly smile - actually I was fervently wishing to be back in Larkhill or Withernsea (or anywhere but Normandy) playing the sax, but at least he got a laugh. Unfortunately within the next twenty minutes he lost both legs to a mortar bomb and died before medics could reach him.

A whistle blew and we were on our feet advancing across a ploughed field toward Bréville. The accuracy of our big guns had effectively kept the defenders' heads down, but their mortaring was as painful as ever. The Shermans continued pounding the village and we crept steadily forward towards our objective. The village was shrouded by smoke - partly due to blazing buildings and partly due to our covering screen. Bill Harrison and I stuck together until a mortar exploded too close for comfort. By one chance in a million I was blown sideways and completely stunned (I discovered afterwards that I broke two fingers) but poor Bill was killed outright - another ex-10th Green Howard gone.

The night became confused after that. I remember dazedly encountering a small Bren group and joining them firing at a blazing building on the outskirts of the village with dim black shapes running all ways and then all went misty. The end must have occurred shortly afterwards as a green Verey light went up and apart from a few scattered shots, all became quiet. The next thing I knew, I was sitting on a low stone wall with a tot of rum in my hand - the good old QM had been following up and the tea dixies were not far behind. Jerry had retreated and the 13/18th, despite some losses, drove through to secure the village. Dead and wounded lay everywhere in the main street and the medical people were busily employed. The battle was ended and Bréville was ours.

Despite the pain in my fingers, I laid down by the wall and slept the sleep of utter exhaustion.

Chapter 12
AFTER THE LORD MAYOR'S SHOW

The first light of dawn revealed the agony of Bréville. Not one house in the village was without damage and several had been completely demolished by the artillery of both sides. A few civilians wandered about, dazedly poking amongst the rubble for goodness knows what. The sounds of war were receding as the Germans fell back to a new defensive position, leaving only casualties and prisoners behind them. By now the 13/18th had regrouped and were on the move through the village to pursue the enemy and the seaborne infantry units were plodding in their wake. Ambulances were in constant demand and a small RAMC Field Hospital was being erected nearby. The Pioneer Corps were also in evidence, collecting bodies for identification and setting up a mortuary in the half-roofless church.

I sat on a stone wall with a few of B Company and as the sun rose we watched the activity with a cigarette and a mug of hot tea - yes, the good old QM had turned up trumps again.

After a scratch breakfast from the remains of our K rations, we paraded for roll call and then moved into the forest on the eastern outskirts of the village. The Independent Parachute Company and the 1st Royal Ulster Rifles took over the village acting as garrison troops and defence force. The main road through, after being cleared of rubble, was now alive with troops, tanks, guns and supplies, all moving in a south-westerly direction and with Military Police putting up Unit signs and controlling the convoys.

In the woods we were issued with sleeping bags from a three-tonner and as the morning sun climbed higher in the sky, we rolled into them and slept soundly under the trees.

In the evening we learnt the facts and figures of the assault. Our CO, Lt Col Johnson, had been killed and in the rifle companies only one officer remained alive (Captain Sims). The total Battalion strength was now down to nine officers and one hundred and fifty-three men. Colonel Parker, despite his mangled fingers, had taken over command of the Battalion in the latter stages and was now acting CO despite his superior rank.

The capture of Bréville had ensured that the 6th Airborne Division had fully completed its bridgehead and were now firmly holding the line from Le Plein to the Bois de Bures. The Division had halted for a breather. But the enemy was not in headlong flight, merely falling back on pre-arranged defence positions.

It was rather an anticlimax but we settled down resignedly to the humdrum chores of digging slit trenches (and latrines), checking arms and equipment and generally pulling ourselves together. Mobile baths and laundries arrived together with reinforcements from the UK. Although most of these wore the red beret, they had done no parachute training (and in fact had arrived by sea), but the numbers brought the Battalion up to strength and as no parachuting was required at this time it didn't really matter - we were now a very cosmopolitan organisation.

The hot summer sun filtered through the trees and mail and rations (including beer) arrived with pleasant regularity. The Signals platoon were nearby and in the evening occasionally the crackle of voices and the burr of static would give way to the soulful sound of Lale Anderson:

> "Vor der Kaserne bei dem großen Tor
> Stand eine Laterne und steht sie noch davor
> So wollen wir uns da wieder seh´n
> Bei der Laterne wollen wir steh´n
> Wie einst, Lili Marleen.
> Wie einst, Lili Marleen."

Strangely enough I met Lili Marleen in person at Nordeney in 1951 and found her to be an ill-tempered, arrogant creature - not at all like the beautiful, seductive temptress we had all visualised!

Squadrons of rocket-firing Typhoons continually roared overhead on their way to blast the German positions and the invading armies. British, American and Canadians numbering in their thousands poured through Bréville - infantry, armour and artillery, all moving steadily forward in a masterpiece of organisation. The weather was hot and we worked stripped to the waist most days. The real enemy at that time were the ever-present mosquitoes (not the planes - the insects!). They attacked by the million, especially at dusk, and several of our lads reported sick with swollen limbs and faces, but there was little the MO could do apart from issue ointment which didn't help much.

On the battlefront, Montgomery's 21st Army Group were advancing on the northern flank of the invasion armies and making steady progress. The 6th Airborne Division were temporarily static. On July the 15th the great man visited Division to present decorations for gallantry (I didn't receive one, needless to say).

Then at last on 17th August we got the word to move. It was raining as we packed out kits, drew ammunition and loaded our airborne carts (very similar to Boy Scouts trek carts except for the contents). We left our (by now) comfortable positions and took to the road as ordinary infantry. The weather had broken and we commenced a dismal trudge through the mud.

Against light opposition 5 Para Brigade moved towards the east. Several German strongpoints remained and caused a lot of inconvenience but not not many casualties. One determined SS Unit were holding a stone farmhouse on the brow of a slight rise and their light artillery, backed by mortars and Spandeaus, were causing havoc. It was several hours before they surrendered, after being blasted by our self-propelled guns and pounded by mortars. Fifteen weary SS Waffen emerged under a white flag with hands up.

A trigger-happy Bren gunner opened up on them and they all died.

Several minor actions like this took place but accidents claimed a few victims also. Three men were killed when sleeping under a tank to shelter from the rain. Earlier than expected the tank moved off, leaving a pattern of blood and crushed bones. A Don R[2] skidded into a stone wall in a small hamlet and demolished both the wall and himself. In a cottage abandoned by its owners, an unsuspecting reinforcement corporal picked up a booby trapped Luger and blew and arm and half his face away, looking for souvenirs.

Eventually we reached the banks of the Seine and dug in. We stood to that evening and next morning the rumours were beginning to fly. We were going home. This was the buzz but none of us really believed it. After all, we had only been in action for less than three months and the Eight and First Army boys had slogged it out for years. This was impossible - but it was true.

The official announcement came from our Company Commander at midday. 6th Airborne Division, having completed their task, were now dropping out of the conflict for the time being and were returning to England for reforming. Later, of course, they would be required again but, for now, it was back to Wiltshire.

It was a wet, squally morning as the Dakota sloshed along the temporary runway and reluctantly lifted itself into a grey sky. At three thousand feet we hit rainclouds and took a bit of a buffeting, but neither rain nor turbulence was to spoil the day. Water bottles illegally filled with rum passed surreptitiously and as the channel convoys passed below the wing like ants floating in soup, we roared the paratroop songs.

> "Come sit by my side in a Whitley,
> Do not hasten to to bid me adieu,
> Just remember the poor parachutist,
> And the job he is willing to do."

Many parachutists willing to do that job were now lying in the soil of Normandy and many more were mutilated for life. But we were the lucky

---

[2] Don R is the military abbreviation for Despatch Rider.

ones - for the time being at least. Who knew what tomorrow would bring? In the meantime forget it - sip the burning spirit and think of today.

The Dakota slid into a shallow descent and the green-brown fields of England loomed nearer.

The trumpets had sounded.

Plumstead Common, London (1934)

Woolwich, London (1936)

Woolwich, London (1938)

Northallerton, N. Yorks (1940)   Richmond, London (1941)

Band of the ITC Green Howards marching past at the opening of the
Church Army Hut, Richmond Hill, London (1940)

Brancepeth, Co. Durham (1946)

Jim with Brindy
Morecambe, Lancs. (1947)

Durham Light Infantry band
Brancepeth Country Fayre Dance (1948)

Annfield Plain, Co. Durham (22nd December 1948)

South Grove, Ryton, Tyne & Wear (1948)

Jim with Best Man Ray "Pussy" Priest (1949)

Royal Tank Regiment Band, Bovington, Dorset (1950)

Joyce outside Married Quarters
Bovington, Dorset (1950)

Northern Ireland (1961)

Northern Ireland (1961)

Jim, Northern Ireland (1962)

BOOK TWO

Chapter I
FAREWELL TO THE SKIES

The aircraft came round into the wind and made a perfect touchdown on Hurn Airport. A cool wind was blowing as we deplaned and marched towards the line of trucks parked on the perimeter of the airfield. After the usual chaos of sorting our gear was over, we climbed aboard and, with a grinding of gears, set off for Larkhill.

Normandy and its horror was behind us, but certainly not forgotten. It was great to be back on English soil again and the countryside had never looked better. Morale was high (probably partly due to the now empty rum-cum-water bottles) and every female from eight to eighty was the target for wolf whistles, cat calls and a host of ribald remarks from the cheerful convoy.

On arrival we were paraded and shepherded into a small canvas 'city'. Our former luxury homes were now occupied by a Battalion of Free French Infantry, awaiting their turn to 'go home' and join in the massive struggle.

Next day we were sent on seven days well-earned leave. The night we returned, it was pouring, the ground soggy and the tents soaked. But next morning the sun emerged, as if to welcome us back to Wiltshire.

The Military round now resumed and we stated weapon training, route marches, range training and even made one Balloon drop at our old familiar DZ at Bulford.

After our recent combat experiences this seemed like going back to school again, but there were two good reasons for this. In the first place, we could not just sit around and do nothing and secondly, drafts of new men were being posted in regularly and needed this training. The 6th Airborne Division was still very much in existence and rumour had it that the next objective was to be the crossing of the Rhine. In late October 1944, we did the first exercise as a Battalion. We were tasked to emplane at Durrington, fly to the outskirts of Bristol and there to drop onto an imaginary enemy airfield (strongly defended by the Home Guard), capture it and then force march back to Camp - a distance of nearly eighty miles!

The drop and the attack were uneventful - even though "Dads' Army" fought to the last pint of bitter!

As we loaded the used 'chutes aboard the truck for their return to Larkhill, I suddenly blacked out and must have fallen off the tailboard as I came round flat on my back on the grass. The Medical Officer was called and after making sure that no damage had been done, ordered me to report to him immediately on return to Camp. I still however had to do the march back, which proved to be a nightmare.

After a hot meal, we fell in by Companies, with the CO at the head of the Battalion and set off. The first ten miles were not too bad, with "Lili Marleen" and "The White Cliffs of Dover" ringing out through the sleeping villages, but gradually the singing subsided and eventually died away, despite the efforts of the Sergeant Majors and NCOs. One by one, men fell out by the roadside exhausted. Gradually the marchers dwindled as following transport picked them up. By this time many of us were wishing we were back in Normandy! To add more pleasure to the situation it began to drizzle with rain, which persisted throughout most of the night. By the time Larkhill was in sight, there was a long straggling file of weary men stretched halfway across Salisbury Plain.

The march had taken us twenty three hours - including rests.

We were given two days rest and then resumed work. I reported sick to the MO as ordered. He gave me a thorough examination, but found nothing physically wrong. Then he asked me if I had any other symptoms. I told him that I had been having slight spells of giddiness, headaches and was sleeping badly. Without another word he picked up the phone and made an appointment for me with the Army Psychiatrist at Salisbury.

This was an odd experience. I had visualised myself lying on a plush couch in the best Hollywood traditions listening to soothing voices, but all I got was a hard chair to sit on in front of a regulation six foot table covered by an Army blanket. The man himself I can clearly remember. He was a middle-aged Major with sharp blue eyes and greying hair curling over his collar. His manner was mild and polite as he asked me many questions (into which I could find very little significance). A few simple tests followed by more questions terminated the examination and I returned to Camp slightly puzzled by the whole business.

Nothing more happened for a few days when the MO sent for me and informed me that I was to appear before a Medical Board at Bulford on the following week.

I presented myself at the Medical Centre at Bulford on the due date. When my turn came, I was directed to a chair in front of a table at which sat three RAMC Officers, a Colonel, and two Majors. I noticed my medical history sheets, the MO's notes and the psychiatrist's report on the table in front of them. They conferred together in low tones and then the Colonel looked at me and smiled.

"Winder, I'm very sorry to have to tell you this, but I'm afraid there will by no more parachuting for you as you are suffering from (a long strange medical word - but which related to a disruption of the mind)."

"Also we have been forced to medically downgrade you to B2, which will obviously mean a posting from your present regiment. It goes without saying that this is no shame or disgrace to you, as we are well aware you have an excellent soldiering record and you are no in any way a unique case as many men have returned from the fighting with this trouble. It will clear up in time and your giddiness and other symptoms will disappear."

"Please report back to your Unit now and good luck to you in the future."

I stood up, saluted and returned to Camp. He was right of course, nobody in a Parachute formation could be other than Grade A1.

So ended my association with the Twelfth Parachute Battalion of the 6th Airborne Division.

Chapter 2
A SEASIDE HOLIDAY

On a war November afternoon I detrained at Bridlington in Yorkshire. Bleary eyes and staggering under the weight of full equipment, kitbag and suitcase, I made for the RTO Office on the station. It wore the depressed look of all wartime stations. Signboards all blanked out and faded posters tempting one and all to holiday in the sunniest spa in the north. There seemed to be a distinct lack of sun as I gloomily awaited transport.

After my medical downgrading, nobody in power at Larkhill seemed to know what to do with me, so I just sat around whiling away as much time as possible in the NAAFI, dodging fatigue parties (at which I was an expert) and the rest of the time lying in the tent reading. Just as I thought that the Army had forgotten me, I was summoned to the Orderly Room and given marching orders. Posted to No. 4 Infantry Training Centre in Bridlington.

Yorkshire again - it seemed like going home!

The town itself, a very popular pre-war holiday resort, was practically deserted. Rolls of barbed wire lined the mined beaches (memories of Hythe), closed down funfairs and amusements, very few cafes open (thanks to rationing) and a general air of decay.

The Army had commandeered practically every hotel and house of any size. After reporting in I was assigned to a rather ancient guesthouse not too far from the seafront. I thankfully dumped my kit, found the cookhouse and tucked into spam fritters and chips - standard menu of the British Army in 1944.

I was issued with a new palliasse of straw and four blankets and then promptly set up home in my new abode - shared with four others. The floor was hard and the straw was damp, but I still managed a good night's sleep.

Next morning I joined a platoon and spent a couple of hours on the drill square - a rather bumpy field on the outskirts of town. A few dilapidated huts and a makeshift range turned out to be the nerve centre of 4 ITC. The interesting afternoon was spent learning how to assemble and dismantle a bren gun, in company with several other D-Day veterans. If this was to be the pattern of my future existence it didn't exactly fill me with ecstasy. There had to be something better than this I thought. In the evening, I found it.

Sitting in one of the few pubs, drinking alone, I suddenly caught sight of a face from the past. It was an ex-Green Howards bandsman "Dinty" Moore. Dinty had been a brilliant trombonist and a very fine musician and his brother "Sally" Moore was formerly Bandmaster of the 1st Battalion the Somerset Light Infantry. Dinty himself however had never risen above the dizzy rank of Lance Corporal, due no doubt to his forthright independent nature.

As we imbibed deeply, I discovered the reason for his presence here. After one of his many clashes with Bandmaster Lester, he had in a fit of rage gone straight to the dentist and had every tooth in his head extracted. This move of course had completely finished his playing days. Chippy Lester, furious at the loss of his solo trombonist, had then kicked him out and here he was!

Dinty, ever the opportunist, had then procured himself a cushy little number as NCO i/c dining hall and was in the process of forming a dance band here with himself as Bandmaster and chief coach. He was overjoyed to see me as the embryo band needed another saxophonist. Needless to say I was only too happy to oblige!

I duly joined the band on the following evening and found myself playing second alto. The lead alto was a former 'pro' who had suffered a shattered leg on the Normandy beaches. On tenor sax was an easy going enthusiastic Captain, who although a hopeless instrumentalist, was nevertheless a good form of insurance on the military side. Due to this gentleman we became a privileged group and bypassed many parades, fatigues and other unpleasant chores of the military life.

The combination, for which there was no name, was twelve strong and was comprised of former musicians both civilian and military. We practiced every evening, making sure we finished before the pubs shut, and also some afternoon. We played for dances in the huge ballroom and for concerts on the stage of the adjoining theatre. On one occasion we backed a show featuring the stars from the immortal Tommy Handley radio success ITMA (It's That Man Again) Senõr So-So and Mrs Mopp (you have probably never heard of them, but I can assure you they were very funny indeed). The house was packed and all went swimmingly well until the final item - the National Anthem.

Unfortunately we had not rehearsed this item and although the military arrangement is in one key, the orchestral version is in another. Being of mixed heritage, we each played out own key. The resultant cacophony was awful and poor red-faced Dinty furiously waved us to a halt. His hissing remark was clearly audible in ever corner of the silent auditorium.

"B FLAT you bloody idiots!"

The troops loved it and gave us a standing ovation.

The stay in Bridlington became a pleasant interlude and I spent a very happy Christmas there. My current lady-love sent me a parcel of 'goodies' which included cigarettes, chocolate and razor blades - all in short supply in war-time Britain, plus a pair of home-knitted khaki socks which would have reached to my chest if I could have got them on!

Training eased off a little as the Yuletide spirit took over. Dinty, who was close friends with most of the local publicans, made sure that the band got its fair share of liquid refreshments and what he couldn't supply them, then our tame Captain certainly could. Taking it all in all, it was a memorable Christmas.

But life is not all beer and skittles and the miserable New Year of 1945 crept unwelcome across the Yorkshire Moors. Training and Exercises started again where it had left off. Drafts came and went with great rapidity, for now the fighting in Europe was reaching its climax and although the Allies had suffered a temporary setback in the Ardennes, Monty was now counter-attacking strongly in the north with his 21st Army Group and the Americans, having recovered from their bloody nose received from Von Rundstedt in the Battle of the Bulge, were now driving enthusiastically for the German homeland. In the East, the Red steamroller was remorselessly crushing everything that stood in its way to Berlin.

None of this was affecting us too much and the band played on. I had acquired a second-hand, ancient clarinet and was doubling sax and clarinet. Not only that, but Dinty had fiddled me onto his "staff" and I was happily scrubbing tables GS as a full blown dining hall orderly. Life was great, but in my heart I knew it couldn't last. How right I was!

In early February the call came. I was called to the Orderly Room and with a sinking heart, heard my sentence.

Posted back to Richmond 5 ITC for attachment to the Green Howards Band! I wasn't too surprised at the posting back to the Depot, after all I as still in the Regiment and I could also see clearly what the resourceful Mr Lester had in mind, because it stood out a mile that he had engineered this diabolical bit of work. His best men were call ups and on the termination of hostilities would melt away like snow in July - he needed every Regular he could lay his hands on - even third-raters!

Richmond was pretty much the same as I had left it three years earlier. The band wasn't much different either - one or two new faces by mostly originals who were riding out the war to a close. At my initial interview Chippy decided that one in oboe in the band was sufficient and henceforth I would dwell amongst the lowliest of clarinet players. It followed that on all the interesting and paid jobs I was not required, but had to stay behind in Richmond with the bandboys and other also-rans.

This suited me not one little bit and it was small wonder that I cast my eyes around for escape.

I heard on the musical grapevine that the Durham Light Infantry were badly in need of woodwind (they had the pick of the brass from colliery bands) and, taking a chance on being hanged for mutiny, I wrote to the Bandmaster at Brancepeth offering my (not very valuable) services. Much to my astonishment he replied at once, offering me a position if I could (a) square Records and (b) square Chippy. Squaring Records was easy enough - after all they didn't care very much, but the thought of my coming interview with the little fire eater filled me with much apprehension.

However I needn't have worried. Although I had improved considerably over the past few weeks, I was still no star and Chippy agreed to let me go. I liked to think that deep down in his heart he sympathised with me, but it was more likely that he had an old score to settle with the BM of the Durhams. I found out later that they were classmates at Knellar Hall in pre-war days!

Chapter 3
BANDS, BANDS AND MORE BANDS

The atmosphere at Brancepeth was completely different. The 1st Battalion Durham Light Infantry Band, small in numbers, consisted of the usual miscellany of boys and ancients, comfortably billeted in the Village Hall of this delightful little hamlet. Close by, along a little winding path, was the Castle of Brancepeth, which dated back to the 12th Century.

My new Bandmaster, Mr Frederick Rippon ARCM, was of rather forbidding facial appearance due to a botched job of mastoid surgery performed by a Army Doctor in pre-war China. A brilliant clarinettist in his day, he could now only blow the instrument with the aid of an assistant holding a hand over half his mouth and supporting the mouthpiece in the other half! This embarrassing task fell to me on one or two occasions and, I must say, I didn't enjoy it at all!

Apart from this he was a thoroughly efficient conductor, a good musician and a likeable fellow despite his rather stiff manner. I think he must have taken a shine to me as I went from second clarinet to solo clarinet in a matter of days! Not a very great honour as it turned out, perhaps because I found it difficult to cope with the parts even though we stuck to very easy pieces. A dance band of sorts was functioning and I was enrolled as second alto sax.

We did a few engagements of a minor nature like concerts in the canteen of Consett Iron Works and Aycliffe Ordnance Factory, but on the whole our world consisted of dull drill parades and dances. The Green Howards Band had been far superior, musically speaking, but I was quite happy in my new station. Durham City, with its pubs, shops, cinemas and a superb ice rink, was only a twenty minute bus ride away. After a few months I was astounded one day to find that I had been promoted to Lance Corporal!

In the DLI Band (I think also in the Guards), it was a Regimental custom for junior NCOs to wear two stripes instead of the conventional one and it was not possible to tell a Lance Corporal from a full Corporal by his sleeve - only from his paybook! Flushed with power, I strutted around like a peacock for days, issuing orders to all and sundry. But it soon fell flat, especially when the orders were completely ignored!

The War had reached its conclusion in the meantime and the infamous thousand year Reich was smashed to a thousand pieces. VE Day was celebrated madly all over the country and especially in County Durham. I spent this historic day in the company of an ex-Green Howard bandsman - Micky Wallace. Micky, who lived in the nearby village of Stanley, took me on a boozy tour of most of the pubs and clubs of nearby Tow Law. It was a wonderful day and the big-hearted Geordies took me to their bosom in no uncertain way. Perhaps it was the uniform, perhaps my Cockney accent, but in no time at all I was completely awash with Newcastle Amber Ale. Although I could only understand about a tenth of their speech, I could see that they were an honest, sincere and hospitable people - this opinion has never changed.

Peacetime had arrived and the wheel commenced to turn again. A week later Freddy Rippon, almost with tears in his eyes, informed four of us - three clarinets and a cornet - that we were to be transferred to the 2nd DLI Band, at that moment being reformed in Sedgefield - 20 miles away.

Off we went in a 15 cwt truck and made our temporary home in a damp Nissen hut situated in a field just off the Stockton-On-Tees road. Our new band consisted of all regulars newly returned from Europe where they had been entertaining troops of 21 Army Group just prior to the end of hostilities. They were due to return there and naturally we would go with them. They had been hit by demob and I was surprised to find it was almost a brass band! There was just one clarinet player (Frank Mirley) and one flute/piccolo (Band Sgt Arthur Plumley), so now all told there was a total of four very moderate clarinettists. The former Bnadmaster, Frankie Rose, who had been a very popular figure in the Regiment, had now retired and his temporary replacement was a former Lancashire Fusilier, "Mad Bill" Elliot.

This was no idle nickname and we were all convinced that he actually was barmy. He would stand at the rostrum with his prominent pale blue eyes gazing into another dimension and wax eloquently for hours upon some peculiar subjects. It would probably start with the life of a famous composer and end up in the realms of astronomy and life in outer space. Needless to say, very little practice would take place and it was a blessing that we only had one job all the four months I was with him.

On New Year's Day 1946 we embarked in a troopship at Tilbury after a bitter cold night in a packed transit camp and, after dodging the mines, arrived in Ostend. There we spent an equally cold night in another packed transit camp. The following day we loaded all our instruments and kit into a goods wagon and entrained for an unknown destination.

It took days to reach Hamburg what with diversions, breakdowns and stops for meals in trackside dining sheds. The scene from the train windows was stark and grim. Hardly any building remained intact and some of the villages were completely flattened either by shelling or bombing.

The crossing of the River Weser turned out to be quite an experience. We had stopped for a meal on the west bank at dawn and here, by coincidence, I recognised one of the Military Police patrolling the line. It was ex-drummer boy Jackson of whom I spoke about earlier. After a few minutes chat I had to get back on the train again. The temporary bridge spanning the wide river was a rickety single track and looking out of the carriage window one could see straight down forty feet into the water. Crossing to the other window the view was the same! Lots of debris and dead animals floated down stream and we were thankful to reach the other bank without joining them. Hamburg Altona station had been very badly knocked about with large holes in the roof and gaps in between the rails through which you could see the street below. The place was packed with refugees of all sorts and the few trains running were tightly jammed and festooned on the outside with travellers clinging onto any and every available handhold. Germany was indeed in a sorry state and even now they were still digging bodies out of the debris.

We changed onto an even slower train and eventually arrived at our destination - Schleswig.

The town was comparatively undamaged due perhaps to its proximity to the Danish border and its lack of military targets. We were billeted in an old castle - the Schloß-Gottorf on the edge of the town, formerly an SS training centre but now housing the Rifle Brigade. The huge room we were given was ancient, dirty and cold. We were allotted double wooden bunks alive with bugs and then promptly forgotten. Mad Bill and his two Sergeants occupied more comfortable accommodation in another part of the the building. Being the only junior NCO, I was in charge of the room and had quite a few tussles with the old sweats just to keep the place clean and tidy.

It was in this small town that I first encountered the "Schwarzhandel" or Black Market. One particular part was always crowded with vendors openly flogging everything from fur coats to Iron Crosses for the real currency of the period - cigarettes. Money was also offered, as much as 50 Reichmarks for a packet of twenty (we could buy our week's ration of 200 from the NAAFI for 8 Reichmarks). So really we could have become instant millionaires but for two things - firstly there was nothing to buy and secondly the number of Marks exchangeable into Sterling at the channel ports was very small (as far as I remember, about £10).

The shops were absolutely empty except for the bakers where long queues patiently waited. A few cafes remained open with small orchestras and fawning waiters who fought furiously for the privilege of emptying the ashtray in the hopes of a couple of butt ends. The only refreshment available in these fading establishments was bowls of watery cabbage soup on coupons and the foul-tasting non-alcoholic beer which Hitler had decreed that the nation would drink.

Fortunately for us all, the NAAFI 'liberated' a large German brewery and started to make beer - very strong and more to the true German style, but unfortunately for the Germans they couldn't have any - only the Allied troops. An old building was turned into a big beerhall and fancifully named 11th Armoured Division Club. The beer was sold at 3d (1p) a pint and after two pints you could feel the hairs on your scalp standing up! Every night gangs of drunken Allied soldiers roamed the streets looking for women and German civilians to rough up and, although the Military Police did their best, it was best to keep a low profile and get off the streets.

There were of course other clubs open to us - the CWL (Catholic Women's League), the YMCA and the RAF's Malcom V Clubs, but they sold nothing stronger than tea.

At the beginning of February we moved again, this time 25km north to Flensburg. It was a little better here and we were more comfortably housed in the former Kreigsmarine Barracks at Glucksburg on the river. Access into the centre of Flensburg was only by ferry boat - unless of course you fancied a very long walk. At night it was hilarious to watch the drunks trying to catch the last boat from the Town Quay. One or two nasty accidents resulted through inebriated Riflemen trying a long jump and missing the boat altogether.

One of our bandsmen, John Sowerby and myself had managed to obtain two sailing dinghies and we spent many happy hours in the perfect early spring weather drifting around on the Flensburgerforde, sometimes reaching the Danish coast, but never being allowed to land. It was in Flensburg that we performed our one and only concert of the tour to a handful of bored troops in the NAAFI. Mad Bill, with his mind on higher things, decided to put on Lidzt's Hungarian Rhapsody N°.2 - an absolute nightmare for a good clarinet section, let alone us, but we struggled manfully through to the bitter end to very tepid applause. For this concert, we did no rehearsal.

The next stop on the tour was Munster in the south. Each time we moved the billets seemed to improve and Munster was no exception. The band occupied a large commandeered house in a pleasant suburb, but not too far from the centre of town - now, as in almost every other town, a pile of rubble with a few churches standing intact.

It was here that I learnt the harsh realities of Black Market life. It was common practice, or should I say the accepted way of life, to do a little bartering with the Germans, as you have already seen. Cigarettes, coffee and chocolate were the main saleable items and all sorts of 'goodies' were obtainable. Everybody, including Officers, were in the game, but nevertheless it was still a crime. One evening I unluckily picked the wrong spot. It was still daylight when a German approached me with a lovely gold watch to sell. Instead of transacting the deal on the main road, which was infested with RMP patrols, I manoeuvred him into what I thought was a quiet side street. I was engrossed in admiring the watch - now on my wrist - while the seller was busily stuffing coffee and cigarettes into his briefcase, when I was horrified to find a Rifle Brigade Captain behind me accompanied by four of the Guard with fixed bayonets.

Shoving past me, he grabbed the briefcase and triumphantly produced a packet of Woodbines like a second-rate magician.

"Ah - government pwoperty what?"

We were both marched to the guardroom and I was stuck in a cell overnight while the Civil Police collected the civilian. What I hadn't realised was that the illicit trading had taken place directly underneath the windows of the Rifle Brigade Officers' Mess!

Next morning I was given a big rocket by the Company Commander, but by virtue of being a regular soldier, was freed, although had to stand by as a possible witness. I had to go to the CCG court and agonisingly await to give evidence. Fortunately I didn't get called. The poor little German wasn't so lucky - he got twelve months imprisonment.

It all proves that life can be very trying, because afterwards I heard from a pal in the Rifle Brigade that the Captain who had pinched me (I cannot mention his name as he was related to the Royal Family) had himself been picked up in Berlin during the previous month for trading coffee (government pwoperty?) for nylons. Of course, due to his connections, the whole affair was discreetly squashed. Very likely he was getting his own back.

A few days later we left the chaos of Germany and returned home.

Chapter 4
THE MELTING POT

Brancepeth Camp was situated on the Durham-Crook road about two miles from Brandon. It was a war-time training centre for the Durham Light Infantry and The Duke of Wellington's Regiment, known officially as 6 ITC.

A large parade ground occupied the centre of the camp with two NAAFIs along one side and a cinema-cum-dancehall along another. There was the usual collection of wooden huts messes and married quarters with plenty of sports pitches and tennis courts. Altogether a very smart, clean and pleasant abode. A quarter of a mile away was the actual village of Brancepeth with its ancient castle mentioned in the previous chapter. It was a reconstruction, originally built in the 12th Century, but in remarkably well-preserved condition. The entrance was through twin towers which formerly supported the massive drawbridge and still kept the huge iron portcullis. Inside there was a well-maintained bridge and two well-kept and well-hated peacocks. The ancient hall to the left of the entrance was now the Officers' Mess and our new home, Russell Tower, was across to the right. The tower consisted of mainly storerooms and workshops on the lower level and limited troops accommodation on the upper floor, reached by a spiral stone stairway. The four rooms allocated to us were connected by a stone-flagged passage. A musty medieval atmosphere hung over the whole place and it was cold, dark and creepy.

By now the nearby village hall had be derequisitioned and was fulfilling its real purpose. Freddy Ripon and his little band of stalwarts had moved away up to the camp, but were dwindling rapidly. In desperation and armed with the CO's approval, Freddy called for volunteers from the recruit squads and, rather surprisingly, netted about ten willing bodies who couldn't tell a bassoon from a mouth organ. It was a bit of a gamble and involved a lot of hard work on his part, but these lads turned out to be very enthusiastic and in later years made the grade as pupils at the Royal School of Music at Knellar Hall.

Our own Mad Bill disappeared somewhere along the way - I don't think anyone know what happened to him, but one day we found ourselves with a new boss - Mr (WO1 Bandmaster) Crowhurst. Immediately he was christened "Spuggy" - the Geordie name for a bird. With much energy he started to make world beaters of us, but our ranks were also being decimated with the dreaded demob disease and it was rather an uphill struggle. We lived in the castle but as there was no suitable practice room there, we practiced in the camp.

It wasn't too long before we finally left the castle, but before we did, I had a strange experience.

It was Whitsun break and the whole band with the exception of four of us were on leave. I was then sharing a room with Hughie Campbell who was also away, leaving me on my own. During the Friday night (or rather, about 3am on the Saturday morning) I woke up to hear loud knocks coming from an ancient cupboard in the room. The uncanny sound continued for a long time and I was petrified with dear. I knew it wasn't the hot water system (there wasn't any) and it couldn't have been a bird (much too strong) and neither could it have been any human agency as there were only about six human beings in the whole castle! I know what you may be thinking, but I had gone to bed completely sober. It was a horrible unearthly sound and I hastily switched the light on, but it still continued. I was too scared to either investigate the cupboard or to flee the room. I just sat and shivered and smoked until daylight, but I must have dozed off because suddenly it was nine o'clock and sunshine. I lost no time in telling the rest of the boys about my "nocturnal supernatural" sound as I called it, but I regret to say they exhibited a strong vein of scepticism in their rather candid observations of the subject. But I am convinced to this day that it as some form of visitation. There was a popular ghost story about a lady in white had been foully done to death in one of the castle dungeons. Several cooks swear that they had seen her floating about down below and one even maintained that he had seen her in the gents' toilets!

We settled in the camp a short distance away from the 1st Bn Band and, although on friendly terms, we were great rivals - especially on the sports fields. Sometimes we joined forces with them, especially on Inkerman Day - the Regimental Day. Most times we shared the duties in the camp, which was an excellent all-round arrangement. Around about this time the 2nd Battalion of the Regiment returned home to the UK from Salonica and amalgamated with the 1st. This now meant that only one band would be required and it was decided to take the best of both and form it into one.

This arrangement went off quite satisfactorily. Freddy Rippon went off into a well-earned retirement and other bits and pieces dropped off conveniently. The National Servicemen awaited their release in a sort of limbo and the also-rans drifted off into other military duties more in keeping with their individual talents. During all this reorganisation and due, I am sure, to some ghastly cerical error, I found myself promoted to Band Corporal.

"Spuggy" became the new boss and here I must put in a quick appraisal of the man.

Mr George Crowhurst was a former Royal Artillery musician and, after an abbreviated wartime course at the Royal School of Music, he became one of the youngest bandmasters in the British Army. He was tall and slim with fair hair and a small moustache, always immaculately turned out, and possessed of a quite manner. A very good brass player (he would often sit with the Dance Band), he had great drive and was exceedingly ambitious. Unfortunately he was rather shy, almost to the point of inferiority complex. In later years he was seconded to a Band in Africa, where he contracted a tropical disease and died - still in the prime of life. A tragic end to a promising career.

But now in 1947 he set about getting some paid engagements for us. I think he must have approached just about every Entertainment Manager at every seaside resort in the north of England He wasn't very successful but we did manage two weeks at Southport, two weeks at Morecambe and several 'day' jobs.

Due to the big reshuffle we found ourselves with an abundance of good clarinet players and I returned to my original instrument - the oboe. But I kept in touch with the clarinet and saxophone, retaining the position of lead alto in the Dance Band, and on the bandstand one of a quartet of clarinets performing Weber's Clarinet Concertino. A bit of a fraud here as our solo clarinet, a grizzled old veteran named Tommy Whittaker carried the three of us on his broad shoulders, but it looked good from down below!

In early 1948 serious romance entered my life in the shape of a pretty little NAAFI girl named Joyce Phillipson. A Tynesider from Ryton (near the famous Bladon), she was a personification of all the virtues I have previously credited to the "Geordies"- kind, smart and a hard worker. With much trepidation I visited her home and met her parents and her six lovely sisters. To my great delight I was accepted and we planned to marry at Christmas.

But before this momentous event the band was due to move to the 1st Battalion DLI at Monkton Farleigh near Bath, for onward move towards Germany. We packed and, with rather heavy hearts, left Brancepeth for the last time.

Our departure from the station was marred by a sad little accident. Many Officers and their families came to bid us goodbye. The Adjutant owned a lively little Spaniel dog who unfortunately found himself on the wrong side of the rails. Seeing his master only a few yards away, he impulsively dashed over the line to him, but unluckily at the moment the train thundered in and the poor little animal disappeared beneath the wheels of the locomotive. It gave us all a nasty turn as we knew it so well. In fact we were nearly at York before we could consider our sandwiches - corned beef!

In this manner I said goodbye to Brancepeth and a delightful interlude in my Army career. Years afterwards I returned on a short sentimental visit - the camp was still there, but long since disused, and weeds, cracked concrete and ghosts were the only occupants. It is now an open cast coal mine with no trace whatsoever of its former military residents.

Chapter 5
GERMANY AGAIN

At Monkton Farleigh we settled into the Battalion but only for a short time as we were scheduled to move to Dortmund in early January. I applied for some leave to get married but only managed to get seven days. The lads had a quick whip round for me and I celebrated my stag night with my two closest friends Frank Mirley and "Pussy" Priest (who was to be my best man).

After a very convivial night on a mixed diet of Bass draught and double whiskies we all staggered up the steep hill to camp, and believe me it was the steepest road I have ever climbed and made more so by the heavy cargo I was carrying. Next morning, feeling very much below par, I travelled north again and we were married in Annfield Plain on a foggy cold day on the 22nd December. After a few days honeymoon in Edinburgh (including a zoo visit on Christmas Day!) I reluctantly took leave of my new wife at Newcastle station. Poor Joyce must have been very agitated as she absent-mindedly tore up her platform ticket and had quite a little difficulty in getting past the ticket collector!

* *   *   *   *   *   *   *   *

Germany was still in ruins, but the first signs of revival were beginning to show. Most of the debris of was was being bulldozed away and a few buildings were being renovated. The Germans themselves were unfriendly and surly, especially while the large steel rolling mills were being dismantled and shipped to Russia as part of the reparations of war.

We occupied a Barracks in the northern suburbs of the city, sharing with the Royal Horse Artillery and support services. We were part of the 2nd Infantry Division and wore the emblem of the Archbishop of York as our shoulder flashes - crossed keys.

Except for the occasional call out of the Battalion on riot duties it was almost a peacetime existence. The Barracks, formerly occupied by a flak unit of the Wehrmacht, was clean and comfortable. The food was good and served up to us by German waitresses. We enjoyed a nice cosy Corporals' Mess and there was the inevitable AKC Globe cinema. Musically it was 'as usual' with drill parades, Officers' Mess concerts and Battalion sports days. This latter meet produced rather an amusing incident in the javelin event. All the mighty throwers, after a ceremonial warm-up, hurled their shafts with much gasping and groanings. At the other end, the German fatigue men retrieved them and casually tossed them back - twice as far!

We put on one concert for the German Civilians - outside the Barracks - but it was so sparsely attended that we never repeated it.

We also travelled to Hamburg to broadcast as "Band of the Week" and enjoyed the break. Ot wasn't the first broadcast for us as we had done three in the UK - two "Music While You Work" (one from Gateshead and one from Bristol) and one on the overseas Forces programme from Newcastle. Altogether we did five programmes and apparently went down well according to the boys in Dortmund - although they may have been a bit biased!

So the days and weeks rolled by swiftly and quite pleasantly. Suddenly it was Demob Day for me, I had now completed my nine years with the colours and it was time for me to do the three on the Reserve. After many celebrations and tearful farewells I left on the military train for the Hook of Holland and the UK. I could have signed on again, and Spuggy begged me to do so, promising me the next vacancy for Sergeant, but being now a married man I had another loyalty, so reluctantly I went.

My military duty was to escort home an ex-Provost Sergeant, busted for drunkenness. "Busty" X (I have forgotten his surname) was one of the meanest looking men I have ever set eyes upon. Six feet something and built like a tank. This was a job I didn't fancy one little bit, but I needn't have worried - he was good as gold and in fact slept most of the way.

I passed through Brancepeth for release documentation and it was then down to Aldershot for civilian clothing. I chose a natty grey pinstripe suit with a red shirt, a purple tie, black shoes and a fawn mac. My taste in clothing had always been suspect and this was no exception!

Chapter 6
CIVVY STREET

Civvy Street hit me like a dose of cold water. I had no job prospects and we were living in my parent-in-law's house in Ryton on Tyne. The first piece of luck came in the shape of a sister-in-law, Maisie, who was secretary to a big Newcastle estate agent. She arrived home one evening and breathlessly announced that she had found us a flat. It was the upstair one of a pair situated in Lemington - just across the Tyne from Ryton. It was old and a bit run-down, but it was not too far from the City. Also the sent was only ten shillings a week (50p). Imagine that today!

In no time at all (with the aid of the family), we scrubbed it, swilled it, redecorated it and filled it was brand new furniture (sadly on hire-purchase). But at least it was ours - our first home.

The second stroke of luck materialised through The Durham Light Infantry Association - of which I was a member. They fixed an interview for me with the Personnel Manager of Messrs. Bainbridge Ltd., a large department store in the centre of Newcastle. Along I trotted, resplendent in best suit and, of course, Regimental tie and presented myself. The great man just happened to be an ex-Major in the DLI, so the result was a forgone conclusion. I got the job and was told to report to the bedding department on the following Monday.

I knew absolutely nothing about mattresses, pillows and beds (except for how to use them of course!) and I stood around looking highly decorative in my best suit, but feeling absolutely useless. It must have dawned upon the management that I was not cut out for the job, but then they made an even ghastlier error by moving me to the haberdashery (drapery) department. This was an absolute nightmare, made worse by two spiteful female colleagues, and I was pleased to escape down to hardware in the basement. Selling pots and pans was only marginally more interesting and I knew in my heart that I had made a very bad mistake in leaving the Army. I could have now been a Sergeant living comfortably in requisitioned luxury in Germany.

Rent and hire purchase repayments were making big inroads into my tiny salary and it became a struggle to live. I could only afford to smoke three cigarettes a day and, up until now, I had been a fairly heavy smoker. But there was nothing left over for luxuries, even though Joyce was a good thrifty housekeeper. I was feeling pretty low when fate dealt me a good hand. Once again, it was Maisie who engineered it.

Due to her connections with the trade, she had discovered a run-down little shop selling fruit, groceries and confectionary. It was situated in the top part of Shields Street (not to be confused with Shields Road, which runs eastwards from the City towards Byker), not far from Sandyford. It was rather a seedy area, not exactly a slum, but heading that way. The shop was going for a song, due no doubt to its grubby and neglected condition. A loan was skilfully manipulated and I very thankfully gave in my notice at Bainbridge's.

This new-found independence turned out to be extremely hard graft. The back shop was three feet deep in mice droppings and the floorboards were rotten. A new floor was built and the dustmen suitably bribed to take away about ten dustbinfuls of rubbish. The front shop was cleared of all the old stock (some of it in rusty tins, years old and quite lethal) and before we could open, we had to stock up completely. Electricity was installed (the place had originally been lit by gas) and everything was scrubbed from top to bottom. I made my mark with the wholesalers and got to know the ins and out of Newcastle fruit market, simply by visiting it at six o'clock in the morning three times a week. This involved getting up at 5 a.m., getting an early bus into town and then wandering around the market looking for the right fruit and veg at the right price. Around eight o'clock I would catch a trolleybus and get to the shop. After a quick cup of tea, the doors would open and the business of the day would commence. So it would continue with half an hour's lunch break until close of business at 7 p.m. But that was the end of the day by any means. After Joyce cooked our evening meal, we would spend the rest of the evening counting food coupons, soap coupons and sweet coupons. This was still the age of rationing and I had 52 registered customers. Returns to the Ministry of Food would have to be completed and the day's takings entered into the accounts book, together with the invoices of goods delivered during the day. By this time it would be ten p.m. and the rest of the day was ours! We opened every day, including Sundays (9 until 1) and only Wednesday afternoon was free.

It was hard going and competition was fierce - a large Co-Op was only several yards away. Several "tick" customers were firmly discouraged, as to me this was an entirely negative form of business, but we still managed to keep a few of the faithful. We lost pounds in bad debts.

Christmas 1948 arrived and, although we had little money, at least we did manage to eat well from stock!

By early spring we realised that at this rate it would take about eighty years to make a modicum of profit, it really was like flogging a dead horse. So we decided to get out while the going was good. Distant bugles were still sounding but I was still determined to give Civvy Street a fair chance.

The sale of the shop went quite smoothly and all the interested parties were satisfied, so I joined the dole queue with a clear conscience. This was only for a few weeks because after a few abortive attempts to continue in the grocery trade, I was drafted to the Post Office.

After the preliminary tests and medical, I started a two week course as a Postal Sorter / Postman. Much to my surprise, at the end of the course I passed the sorting test of 1000 letters in 9 minutes with a maximum error margin of 3%. Immediately I was put on the night shift for the first six weeks.

I really hated this business of turning night into day. I would leave the flat at eight o'clock at night and cycle the five miles of notorious highway known as the Scotswood Road into the main sorting office. Dinner break would be from 12.30 a.m. until 1 a.m. and then a further break from 4 until 4.30. It was a monotonous and boring job, the most difficult part of which was trying to keep awake. Sleep during the day was difficult with traffic, dog and children noises to content with.

I first discovered that I was not really Post Office material one early morning when an inspector asked me to take out a round for a missing man. I 'faced' up to the round - which meant getting the letters in street and number sequence - and tied them all into ten bundles. The first snag was the absence of satchels and I was compelled to use a huge red canvas sack instead. All went well until I reached the beginning of the round - a long strung-out area of the City - when I had the misfortune to fall off the bus and, after dropping the sack, all my inadequate ties came apart. 900 letter were now adrift in a hopeless muddle and the next three hours were a nightmare as I darted hither and thither trying vainly to get them into the right letterboxes. To improve matters, it started to pour with rain.

My absence must have been noticed in high places, because around midday a van driven by a puzzled inspector came out to rescue me. Between us we managed to sort everything out and eventually I returned to the office at 1.30 tired and soaking wet, with most of my enthusiasm dampened.

I thought that this episode would have put paid to my career as a walk postman, but strangely it didn't. A week later I left the night shift and was given a regular route. This time I learnt to tie up a little better and get a decent satchel, so I even began to enjoy it (slightly)!

On my new round lay a brewery and after delivering the mail to the office I would be invited by the open-hearted staff to partake of a little liquid refreshment, which I willingly accepted. At the end of a huge shed lined with massive barrels was a cute little nook complete with tapped barrel, glasses and an elderly easy chair. I would thankfully subside into the chair, draw myself a pint, light a cigarette and scrutinise the daily paper - all the GPO problems on another planet. Half an hour later, with several pints aboard, I would stagger off to complete the round. Strange how much easier it then became!

The itch to travel was still with me and I missed the Army very much. I could never see myself as a career postman even though the work was quite easy. I did make the attempt however, even if it was a token gesture to my conscience.

One bright summer's morning after finishing my round, I slipped into a newsagent for the paper. Spotting the 'Melody Maker' on the shelf, I bought it. There under the heading "Musicians Wanted" was my future.

'Rhine Band Royal Tank Regiment now forming, requires experienced musicians. Vacancies on all instruments. Apply Director of Music, Bovington Camp, Dorset.'

In a flash, I did.

Understandably there was some coolness from the family when I announced my intentions of rejoining the Colours, but there was no stopping now. A few days after making my application a telegram arrived from Bovington offering me paid Lance Corporal with married quarters available.

We sold most of the furniture and Joyce moved back to her home across the Tyne. Another sister, Peggy, and her husband Les took over the flat and with suitcase packed, I took the train south.

Chapter 7
LIFE WITH MY BOY WILLIE

Bovington, in common with most military camps, was way out into the wilds of Dorset - due no doubt to the wide open spaces requirement for armoured vehicles. It was a red hot day when I got off the train at the local station Wool. Not seeing any taxis (indeed I couldn't have afforded one in any case), I trudged up the three miles to the Camp carrying the heavy case. By the time I reached the Driving and Maintenance School (where the band was situated), I had worked up quite a sweat.

I reported in to the Director of Music, Lieutenant Bob Jarvis, who greeted me warmly and filled me in on the situation.

There were already two other bands RTR in existence, "Alemain" at Catterick and the original Tank Corps Band "Cambrai" right next door to us at Bovington. As the Royal Tank Regiment now consisted of eight regiments of tanks (most of them in Germany), it was decided to form a third band solely to cater for them. The Rhine Band was about a month old when I joined them and consisted of transfers in from other bands plus a proportion of talented youngsters directly from civilian life. Personnel of the band when I joined them on 1st September 1950 were as follows:

FLUTE:	Cpl. Jimmy Barr (R. Hampshires)
OBOE:	Band Sgt. Major Maxie Mayland (14/20 Hussars)
CLARINETS:	Sgt. Johnny Hiorns (Rifle Brigade)
	Cpl. Bill Lyall (KDG)
	Bdsm. Gus Woods (Direct Enlistment)
	Bdsm. Ron Jordan (DE)
	Bdsm. Ron Bailey ((DE)
	Bdsm. Gordon Peach (DE)
	Bdsm. Brian Naden (DE)
	Bdsm. Fred Harvey (DE)

	Bert Yeatman (Cambrai)
ALTO SAX:	L/Cpl. Jim Winder (DLI)
TENOR SAX:	Bdsm. Rocky Knight (DE)
BASSOON:	Bdsm. Jim Burgess
CORNETS:	Bdsm. Ted Robyns (DE)
	Bdsm. Ray Jannaway (DE)
	Bdsm. Steel (DE)
	Bdsm. Crane (DE)
HORNS:	Cpl. Chapman (KRRC)
	Bdsm. Don Chappell (DE)
	Bdsm. John Crackle (DE)
EUPHONIUM:	Bdsm. Ginger Silver
TROMBONES:	Sgt. George Lock (R. Berks)
	Bdsm. Mick Chiesman
	Bdsm. Norman Dennett Lockwoord
BASSES:	Bdsm. Johnny Hunt (Camrai)
	Bdsm. Frank Taylor (East Lancs)
DRUMS:	Bdsm. Albert Sands (11 Hussars)
	Bdsm. Larry Dinmore (RAF)

The Regimental March was a folk song entitled "My Boy Willie" and was very popular as it lent itself to all kinds of homemade lyrics!

I was issued with a brand new oboe - valued at £250 - which was quite a large sum in those days. But it was hard going as I had done no serious practice since leaving the DLI, although I had played with the Northumberland Youth Orchestra and the Stanley Symphony Orchestra on occasions. However the oboe is not an instrument to be trifled with and constant practice is really important. The result was that my lips swelled up so much that after a day or two I could hardly blow a note. The D of M, seeing this, decided to transfer me back onto Alto Sax, on which I managed fairly well. Eventually I went back on to oboe but it was months later, in fact, when we were in Germany again.

Married Quarters (mainly consisting of converted WW1 wooden huts) were fairly plentiful and I managed to secure an A type, that is a one bedroomed one in Elles Road. I took a little leave and brought Joyce back to her new home. The hut stood well back from the road and we shared with a C type (three bedrooms). Front and rear was a hideous tangle of weeds and brambles laughingly known as gardens. The interior was austere to say the least. Heating arrangements in the living room consisted solely of an old fashioned American stove with a tiny grill to provide heat and all the cooking also had to be done on this monster. The huge iron kettle took an age to boil, so there was no such thing as a quick cup of tea! Bath night was hard work as this involved lighting a fire beneath a huge boiler in the bathroom and ladling the hot water into the bath as it boiled. The whole house was tastefully decorated in a pleasant workhouse green, supplemented by a rich manure brown.

Yes, even in 1950 our Quarter was a little behind the times!

* *   *   *   *   *   *   *   *

As I settled down in the band, so Joyce got to know some of the other band wives - later on she was to know them in more detail. The atmosphere was pleasant as we were all new boys and no cliques had yet formed. Christmas 1950 saw us all dispersed to various localities on leave - naturally we went to Ryton.

Early in 1951 I decided to study for the Forces Preliminary Exam. Partly with the view that it may come in handy later and partly with the fact that this was pre-television days! I took the exam on a freezing cold May day in 1951 in the Gymnasium - that night I played at a dance in the same hall! Some months later when I was in Berlin I learnt that I had passed Parts 1 and 2 in the same examination and apparently was the only one in Southern Command to have done this.

Around this time we found that we were going to have a family and we were both overjoyed. The forecast date was December and it was going to be the first Grandchild so Father and Mother in-law were quite pleased.

The band was improving daily. Probably it was the talent of the younger members together with the experience of the others that activated this.

Psychologically of course, the fact that we were a Staff Band and therefore a cut above all others may have helped!

In May we heard, as expected, that we were due for a two year tour in Germany - initially being attached to the 5th Royal Tank Regiment at Hohne. Although based at Hohne, we would of course be continually visiting all the RTR in Germany and also the Independent Tank Squadron in Berlin. At this time the 2nd and 6th were also in Munster, the 1st in Detmold and the 8th in Paderborn. The 3rd and 4th were in the Middle East and the 7th in the UK.

In July we left Bovington to the Cambrai Band and moved out to Hohne, just north of Celle and close beside the site of the infamous Concentration Camp of Bergen-Belson. All the band wives were left behind as there was a decided lack of Married Quarters in the Hohne Garrison. In fact only two of the band managed to get one and neither of them was me!

We soon settled into Hohne and, despite the lack of Quarters, were quite happy with comfortable accommodation. I shared a room with Bert Yeatman, a pre-War Tank Corps man and an ex-POW, having been captured at Fort Capuzzo in the Western Desert. We developed a good friendship which was to last many years. Meantime, back at Bovington, Win Yeatman was busy looking after Joyce's pre-natal warfare.

Band work at Hohne consisted of the usual tasks - drill parades, Officers' Mess and troops' concerts for 5 RTR with occasional ventures beyond.

September saw us in places as far apart as Nordeney, Bad Oeynahausen and Berlin.

We had a glorious two weeks leave on the holiday island of Nordeney in the Baltic. It was also a British Army Leave Centre (with a nudist camp thrown in for good measure!).

Within a few days (in fact just enough time to collect the mail and clean laundry) we were on our way to Bad Oeynahausen - the then HQ Rhine

Army (later removed to Mönchengladhach) - and there played for a Royal Signals parade in nearby Lemgo with HRH Princess Royal taking the salute. After a further evening concert in Bad Oeynahausen we boarded the night train for Berlin.

Here we spent a fascinating month. We were billeted in the dressing rooms of the massive Olympic Stadium with three Olympic class swimming pools in our back garden! The weather being red hot, we really cashed in on this good fortune. Relations between the occupying Western Powers and the civilian population were very cordial, no doubt due to the recent Berlin airlift in which a shuttle service of planes flew essential supplies of food and fuel into the beleaguered City. Relations were even now cool between the West and the East and the Russians, having failed in their blockade, were still trying to win the hearts of the West Berliners. This was of course before the infamous Wall was erected.

Civilians were friendly to us - quite different to Celle, Hanover etc. and we were allowed free travel on all City Transport.

We played at several notable concerts and parades. The Band of the Inniskilling Dragoons, ourselves and the pipes and drums of the Guards Brigade put on a Tattoo - together with Tanks, Engineer and Artillery Units, in the huge Blumengarten grounds. This was a counter attraction to a huge Communist Rally in East Berlin and it attracted a crowd of almost 30,000 people - mainly from East Berlin.

An even larger crowd turned up at the Waldbuhne - a huge amphitheatre seating 50,000 people, to see a performance of the film "Red Shoes" with Moira Shearer in the leading role. Before the film started we gave a concert in front of the gigantic screen, which was well appreciated.

This led to one of the most embarrassing moments in my career. Just before the show, my good friend Johnny Hunt and I partook of several excellent "Braun" beers and by the time the performance finished we were both desperately in need of a leak. Unfortunately there were no toilets available, so as soon as the lights went out, Johnny and I hightailed it up the steep slope being the screen and there thankfully let go into the darkness. Suddenly, the lights went on again and we were caught good and proper, peeing in front of a very appreciative audience of 50,000 people!

A faint ripple of applause and laughter went up (who said the Germans lack a sense of humour?) and, red-faced, we dropped to the ground to wriggle away from the revealing searchlights. This incident might have had serious repercussions, but in fact was a good laugh for days afterwards.

Lift was very pleasant in Berlin and we thoroughly enjoyed our stay. We did a concert and a couple of parades for the Independent Tank Squadron RTR - but they were the only military jobs. We played at a football match at Spandau where the home side entertained Burnley FC. We were all delighted when Burnley ran out easy winners by four goals to nil.

We sampled the delights of nightlife in the City and many mornings saw us arrive at the Olympic Stadium in dawn's early light. In Mariandomm (U.S. Sector) we played at a concert which was on TV. It was quite exciting to watch on the monitor sets. Around this time we also featured in the magazine 'Soldier' in an interesting little article entitled "Birth of a Band".

Unfortunately all good things come to an end and this trip was no exception. With much reluctance we steamed out of Berlin-Charlottenburg, again to pull down the blinds through dismal East Germany.

Hohne was more or less the same as we had left it, except a little colder. It was now November and we were all looking forward to Christmas leave at home - especially in my case. Joyce had abandoned the "Garden Shed" in Bovington and once more returned to her parents in Ryton-on-Tyne. I really don't know what we would have done without them regarding accommodation, as we had nowhere else to turn to. I am forever in their debt.

In mid-November, Maxie Mayland left us to go to Regimental Duty as Officers' Mess Manager 5 RTR and, in the subsequent reshuffle, George Lock was appointed Band Sergeant Major. Bill Lyall went to subs. Sgt. and I joined Jimmy Barr as a Local (unpaid) Sgt. After thirteen years I was about to enter the golden gates of the Sergeants' Mess! It was unbelievable and, although I was still paid only as a Corporal, at least I was one of the Band elite, in fact I was 6th in command!

In the 15th December a happy Rhine Band poured onto the Hook of Holland leave train at Soltau, thence to a smooth crossing. After smuggling 600 cigarettes past a bribable Customs Officer at Harwich, I eventually reached Ryton at 7 o'clock on the morning of December 17th.

Mother-in-Law was up and about when I arrived, no sign of my wife anywhere around.

"Where's Joyce then? Still in bed no doubt. Well I'll go up and roust her out!" Forced heartiness after a night on the train.

Mother-in-Law gave me a puzzled look.

"Didn't you get our telegram?"

"No, what telegram?" (It arrived in Hohne one after I had left).

"Well you are now a Daddy! Joyce is in Dilston Hall (a maternity home near Hexham) and you have a daughter - one week old!

And that is where Anne came in.

Chapter 8
STILL IN GERMANY

The somewhat early arrival of Anne (she was expected on 22nd December) gave me a slight shock, but the news that I had signed on for another ten years gave Joyce an even bigger one! She burst into tears and I felt awful, but after a time she must have accepted that it was the only life for me and cheered up a bit. Reluctantly bidding them farewell, I left again for Hohne in mid-January 1952.

February '52 saw my first real experience of the internal combustion beast. Bill Lyall and I clubbed together and bought a car from a quickly-posted REME Sgt. It was a huge old American Chevrolet and we had great fun tearing around the quiet roads of Northern Germany much to the horror of the locals. It was an advancement on the tandem trips of a few months earlier, but a lot more expensive (petrol was dear). We soon solved this problem with the aid of a few friends in the Sgts Mess and I'm sure the Centurion tanks didn't notice the loss of a few gallons!

In view of the housing situation it was decided to move the Band from Hohne down to the 8th RTR in Paderborn (Westphalia), as a whole street of new houses were available for us there. This was indeed good news as it meant that eight wives and families would now join us.

Early in March 1952, three three-tonners and a bus pulled out for Paderborn with four of us behind in our Chevy. We had had problems with the core plate of the water jacket and the best brains of the REME with the most ingenious ideas had so far failed to solve the trouble. On our way to Celle we called in at a small country garage and noticed to our dismay that the wretched plug was leaking again. In desperation, we asked the elderly proprietor if he could do anything for us. He nodded slowly and, taking a jack knife from his pocket, strolled over to the nearest tree. Cutting off a small twig, he came back and rammed it into the core plug. That plug never leaked again!

Paderborn was quite different from Hohne. It was an ancient medieval, town thick in history, with a strong ecclesiastical flavour. A massive Dom (cathedral) dominated the centre of the town and dozens of churches (mostly Lutheran) were sprinkled through the narrow streets. There appeared to be no sign of any bomb damage anywhere and very little signs of any industry since agriculture was the principle occupation. Barker Barracks lay about 3km east of the town and was quite a bit older than our previous accommodation, being also a pre-war Panzer Kaserne.

The band occupied the complete top floor of the main barrack block and soon we had settled in. The Sgts Mess was good, but not up to the same standard as in the 5th. Within days, all the married men were allocated a house in Schlaunstraße - a fairly quiet area not far from the station. These Op Union houses, as they were known, were remarkably good little terraced houses with two bedrooms, a cosy lounge, smart practical kitchen and a cellar consisting of a boiler room and two others (I eventually ran a model railway down there!).

We were all highly delighted with these brand new quarters and after a year of bachelorhood we could start living as married men again.

I brought Joyce and Anne over in May 1952 and, although it was Joyce's first visit to Germany (in fact, any country abroad), Schlaunstraße soon became a small English colony and we all became good friends and neighbours.

The band was still busy visiting other Royal Tank Regiments and we were away for days and sometimes weeks at a stretch fulfilling our role of wandering musicians. During these times that we were home, we did manage a few outings to Winterburg (where I did a bit of skiing) and Bad Harzburg (then a leave centre). On one occasion Joyce and I stayed in the palatial Hotel Kompanistenheim, meaning "Composer's Hotel". Franz Lehár, Strauss, Mozart and others had stayed here, so we were in good company. It was an awful place to stay really - high, draughty rooms, poor service and a lingering odour of polish and stale sauerkraut hung about everywhere. I made sure we had a change on the next trip.

We visited Bad Harzburg and Winterburg quite often on duty as they were both leave centres, but it seemed that the Germans appreciated us far more than the British Army!

In August 1952 a rather important event occurred. Despite the fact that we, as a Staff Band, were not officially required to be inspected by the RMSM as were Regimental bands, Jumbo nevertheless volunteered for one. The Commandant plus Director of Music, followed by their retinue, duly arrived in our midst. We fumbled our way through the sight-reading piece (Gordon Jacob's "Festival Overture"), our own set piece (Rossini's "La Boutique Fantasque") and performed the necessary gyrations on the barrack square. At the conclusion of the inspection, thanks to Jumbo's encouragement, I was interviewed by the great men, who accepted me as a future candidate for Studentship at Kneller Hall. This was greatly surprising - normally it was a great fight to be numbered amongst the Bandmasters-to-be. I can only think that there must have been a huge number of vacancies that year!

I immediately started a crash course in harmony and counterpoint, encouraged by Jumbo and assisted by a couple of talented souls, but over the months my enthusiasm waned and died. I couldn't really see myself as a Bandmaster. I was purely and simply an instrumentalist and nothing more. Eventually I steeled myself and told Jumbo this. He was very understanding and sympathetic, but he knew I had the germ of unrest within me and suggested I try for the Royal Army Education Corps. With this in mind, I secured myself an interview with an RAEC Major from District HQ. Despote the fact that I held the Forces Preliminary Certificate of Education, he informed me that it was insufficient qualification for the Corps. I personally knew of many friends within the RAEC who were on their way up although they only held the FPE. I argued with this officious, pompous little popinjay for a time and then finally stormed out of the room.

I walked over to the Regimental Orderly Room and there sat the Chief Clerk, who gave me all the details regarding transfer to the Royal Army Pay Corps (my second string). I duly made application and two weeks later was accepted. I would have to revert from my present rank of

Substantive Sgt. to that of Subs. Cpl. (Acting Sgt.) but later I would get this back again. Rather than lose pay, I would in fact gain B1 Tradesman's rate instead of the non-tradesman's rate I was on now.

Meanwhile, I was still very much in the band and musical duties were keeping me busy. Christmas was approaching rapidly. We went to Hamburg for a week as Band of the Week on the British Forces Network. At Plon School (just north of Hamburg) we did a concert in which I played Saint-Saen's "Dying Swan" as an oboe solo accompanied by Dave Thornett on the piano. This was a little scarifying as it was a live broadcast with no chance of editing out the errors!

Our dashing and genial Band Sgt. Major George Lock organised most of our Xmas Programme and all the single men were entertained in the married quarters. My allocation was Jimmy Barr, Arthur Pinney, Ted Robyns and Lofty Batsford. We held a band social night (in Barker Barracks) and in fact a very good Xmas was enjoyed by all.

Early in 1953 I leant that I had been officially accepted by the RAPC under the Army Council Instructions relating to transfer in as a Unit Pay Clerk. I decided to send Joyce and Anne back to the UK, as they could then settle down a little while I did the sic month course at Devises. Accordingly I booked their passage under the Op Union scheme, but by a quirk of officialdom I had to pay for my own passage return on the civilian ship. Fortunately the whole band were also going home on 28 days leave - except of course for the married men who were remaining in married quarters in Paderborn. We reluctantly handed over our nice little house and left for the UK.

At the Hook of Holland I parted company from Hoyce and the rest of the band and embarked on the British Railways steamer "Duke of York" while they were called forward to the military ship "Empire Vienna".

Being the faster vessel, we left a little after them and were scheduled to arrive in Harwich an hour earlier. I was sharing a four berth cabin aft with a man and his young son. After a few pleasant duty free brandies in the ship's bar, I turned in for the night.

Around four o'clock in the morning I was awoken by a shuddering jar, followed by an ominous silence as the engines stopped. In the sudden hush I heard the stewardess outside in the passage shouting that all was well and there was no need for panic. She opened our door and said quietly:

"Please get dressed quickly and get up on the top deck with your lifejacket - we've had a bad collision and I believe we are beginning to sink!"

* *   *   *   *   *   *   *   *

We didn't sink, however, and on arriving on the top deck I realised what had happened. The "Duke of York" had been rammed just under the bridge by an American PX ship outward bound for Bremerhaven, the "Haiti Victory" (twice our size). It was a mystery how this had happened, as it was broaD-Daylight and both ships we equipped with radar, but it turned out at the enquiry that the whole accident was due to negligent lookouts. In the meantime, however, our complete bow section had been almost sheared off and was hanging by a couple of steel plates.

It was vital that everyone should get off as soon as possible and lifeboats were lowered and filled with women and children. The remaining men were ordered to the top deck and from there we jumped onto the Haiti Victory's main decl. It was quote a perilous leap but fear leant wings and we all transferred safely.

From our new position we could see the situation quite clearly and as we watched, the whole bow section turned over, tore itself loose and began to sink. A young deckhand on his first sea trip, asleep in his bunk, was rudely awakened by the crash. He pulled himself through the now horizontal porthole and clambered onto the side of the ship as it was beginning to submerge.

"Swim for it!" We all yelled.

But unfortunately he was a non-swimmer and floundered ineffectively in the deepening water. The situation was saved by the boatswain of the Duke of York who dived from the bridge to effect a spectacular rescue - for which he received the Distinguished Conduct Medal and a broken arm, but at least it was a life saved.

The whole portion of the ship from just below the bridge to the actual forepeak went down, but the remainder of the ship stayed afloat and was later towed to the Tyne for repairs and a new bow.

* *   *   *   *   *   *   *   *

This little episode made me a mini hero, especially with the sister-in-laws. I received a red carpet welcome when I arrived in Ryton on the following morning, but I think it must have been sheer relief at hearing that I was still in the land of the living and not mouldering on the sea bed some sixty miles off Margate (as Joyce was first informed)! I did nothing except jump onto another ship and leave my case behind, but I even got that back later. But the whole thing did give me a nasty phobia - I never could sleep properly on a ship again, even years afterwards.

I returned to Germany after leave and to a further bachelor existence. We continued on our musical way until our next trip to the UK in August, which was to be two weeks on the Bandstand at Weymouth followed by 28 days leave. The first week we were billeted at Bovington Camp, but found this inconvenient (besides the food at Bovington was terrible), so we moved into the YMCA at Weymouth for the second week. This was my last civilian engagement with a military band and I thoroughly enjoyed it.

Back in Paderborn I was warned that I would be joining Course No. 55 Unit Pay Clerks and to report in November to the RAPC Training Centre. After a great send off party in the Mess I got as far as Dusseldorf when I was summoned by the metallic voice of the station announcer to leave the train and report to the RTO (Railway Transport Officer). Here I found out that in true British Army tradition, they (the powers that be) had put me on the wrong course - it should have been No. 56, not No. 55.

So, complete with hangover and full kit, I had to wend my way back to Paderborn again by slow train. The whole affair was more than a little bit embarrassing.

I did no more blowing now as I had already handed over the oboe to my relief Sgt. "Barney" Steel from the Border Regiment (later to become Band Sgt. Major Rhine Band). I now just kicked my heels and passed the time in minor admin jobs and instructing boys.

One cold morning, as the band were rehearsing Christmas carols, I left once again for the Hook of Holland, but this time there was no mistake about it - I was on my way back. As I turned my back on Paderborn, I was also turning my back on a fifteen year association was Military Bands.

The end of an era, but I didn't look back.

Chapter 9
A NEW LIFE

Any preconceived ideas I had about the RAPC Training Centre being a home from home, with long-haired, down-at-heel clerks slouching about, were rudely shattered when I arrived there on the first day of January 1954. The Camp, consisting of Waller Barracks (RAPC Training Centre) and Prince Maurice Barracks (REME Regimental Pay Office), lay about two miles to the west of Devizes, in the open Wiltshire countryside.

Squads of Regulars and National Servicemen were being drilled by keen young instructors on the three parade grounds, while from the miniature ranges came the crackle of small arms fire. Everything gave the impression of efficiency and military orderliness. This, of course, was the policy in those days, when the RAPC was fighting against civilianisation - soldiers first, clerks second.

A row of antiquated bungalows ran along one edge of the camp by the cinema. It was in one of these the 56 Unit Pay Clerks Course gathered. The course instructor was S/Sgt. "Dougie" Morris, assisted by Cpl. Porteous. We started with five Sergeants and about thirty junior NCOs and finished six months later with two Sergeants and twelve others! The work itself was not too exacting, but the general attitude amongst junior L/Cpls was that it was a shortcut to the Sgts Mess.

The six months included a month at Regimental Pay Office (I went to RAOC Office in Leeds) and a shoer spell at the Officers Accounts Branch Ashton-Under-Lyne. The concluding test was for B1 status, which none of us had much trouble with. We all waited expectantly for our postings and I was hoping against hope to get something in the Middle or Far East, but no such luck - it was Germany once more! 111 Coy RASC in Fallingbostel.

So, in July 1953 I passed through the RAPC Depot at Ash Vale en route for BAOR again. By now I was beginning to lose count of the number of times I had crossed and re-crossed that North Sea. After a brief stay in Command Pay Office at Lubbecke, I moved northwards to 111 Coy RASC.

With three sister Companies (109, 110 and 112), the Unit formed the RASC Transport for 7th Armoured Division - the famed Desert Rats. Each company performed a separate function and ours was to supply petrol, oil and other essential stores to the various formations within the Division.

On arrival I received a moderately warm welcome - not red-hot, but I found the reason for that later. I was lucky enough to be allocated a large, comfortable room in the mess - just over the bar! I shared this with Doug Harding - a young, smart Platoon Sgt.

After a few days I was delighted to hear that I had been allocated a Married Quarter in the Garrison and, during the following month, made the weary pilgrimage across the North Sea once more. Everything went smoothly and we settled into our Garrison Flat with no problems (we even had a pet dog supplied!) and I recommenced work.

On the first morning I was seated at my desk in the Pay Office when an SIB (Special Investigation Branch RMP) Sergeant Major walked in. He showed me an Aquittance Roll, which was a large sheet containing particulars of about a dozen soldiers, together with details of payments to them over the month. He asked me if I thought any of the figures had been altered and I agreed - they had. To cut a long story short, 111 Coy had always had a RASC Sgt. to perform all pay duties, until I arrived as the first RAPC representative. My predecessor in this case was a little cherubic gentleman named Charlie...

Charlie, despite his angelic looks, had been altering the rolls and paybooks for years and had made over £3000 - big money in those days. He was very popular with all the young drivers - handing out subs to them on every occasion, He was also highly popular in the Mess bar with his generosity in treating one and all. Unfortunately they didn't realise it was their own money that they were drinking!

While I had been away in the UK on leave it was in keeping with Charlie's character that he should try and grab the last little bit, but this proved his undoing. I was completely unaware of any discrepancies until two young National Servicemen told me that they hadn't yet been paid. Their paybooks were missing, but according to the rolls they had already been paid - plus credits.

Suspecting them of an attempted fiddle, I reported the matter to the Imprest Holder (Capt. A. H. Blair RASC) and he immediately called in the Military Police, who opened the whole can of worms.

The upshot of the whole matter was that Charlie was court martialled and received twelve months hard labour in Shepton Mallet, followed by an ignominious discharge from the Army. Everyone was most upset, even though he had robbed them systematically over the years!

This then was my start as a Pay Sgt. with 111 Coy RASC and, although there was a perceptible coolness to me after this affair, it soon disappeared and I became quite a popular member of the Company as the months went by.

* *   *   *   *   *   *   *   *

Life in Fallingbostel was very pleasant - if a little claustrophobic. Isolated on the North German Heide as we were, there was only the NAAFI and Fallingbostel Village in which to shop. Hamburg was too far to the north - as was Hannover to the south. A few months of this restriction became a little irksome to us, so I decided to buy a little car in which to get around. Luckily I found what I wanted fairly quickly. Bill Kibble, the huge RSM of our Div. Co.. HQ decided that his old 1936 Opel Olympia was no good to him as he couldn't sit in the driver's seat wearing his cap, so he sold it to me for £25! It was a good, old, solid car, but with a top speed of only about 60kph.

We now started to go a little further afield and spent several holidays outside Germany - Austria, Holland and Denmark. On all these long distances the old Opel chugged slowly and steadily along the Autobahn (overtaken by just about everything in sight), with Anne fast asleep on the back seat. We covered thousands of miles this way and certainly saw our share of the continent. I was rather sorry to see that old car go. Just before my posting home I sold it (now resprayed black) to a Bandsman in the 4/7 RDG, who promptly wrecked it in a few days. No breathalysers in those days!

In 1956 the Suez crisis reared its ugly head and created an awful amount of work. Reservists we recalled to the Colours and the Company inflated to three times its normal strength. I was kept going continuously, assisting these people with their hardship claims and quite often a long queue built up outside the Pay Office patiently waiting their turn. I had a young girl Pay Clerk named Fraulein Schlemme, a refugee from East Germany, but she was totally incapable of dealing with this sort of work - she couldn't even add up! Eventually I was forced to go to the OC for help and was given two former RASC Clerks who, despite their lack of knowledge concerning Pay matters, certainly knew their stuff regarding general clerical duties and were of terrific assistance to me. I also packed a large box with cigarettes, toothpaste, soap and cleaning materials which we hoped to take into the Desert with us. Funnily enough, when we eventually stood down and unpacked the box, it was quite surprising to find a large portion of the contents to be missing. However, as the PRI had financed the enterprise in the first place, no tears were shed.

In the middle of all this chaos, the stork decided to pay us a visit. I was a keen darts player and captain of the mess team. After a home game against the 4/7 DGs I decided to have an early night and it was just as well that I did. It started at midnight and Joyce was on her way to Hannover British Military Hospital by three a.m.

Our second daughter Lynn Joyce was born in BMH at 7.45 a.m. on 5th October 1956.

* *   *   *   *   *   *   *   *

Suddenly the whole affair collapsed in an anti-climax. Diplomatic pressure was applied by the USA and Russia and the French and ourselves were forced to pull out of the Canal Zone, which was a great shame in view of the fact that the Para had made such a good start.

Most of our vehicles had been moved to Marseilles for onward shipment via Cyprus to Egypt. They were now retrieved and returned to Ordnance. The called-back Reservists were stood down and returned to the UK, none the worse for their adventure, and the tropical mid-east clothing and equipment, so hastily issued to us in the first place, was just as hastily withdrawn before some enterprising soul had the opportunity of cornering the market.

Peace descended once again on Fallingbostel.

We managed to secure a slightly larger and brighter flat and moved in. My downstairs neighbour was Reg Neal, Pay Sgt. of 4/7 RDG and we spent many convivial evenings together, both in the Mess and the RAOB Lodge, as I had now been elected to the Order. Time was passing rapidly and once again it was the packing season. This was done as usual by the efficient Joyce.

Our destination was to be the RASC Regimental Pay Office, Blakelaw, Newcastle-Upon-Tyne. We spent disembarkation leave at my in-laws (as always) and at the end of February I duly reported for duty.

Blakelaw Camp was to the north of Newcastle, but it was purely and simply an office and there was no living accommodation of any sort there. Every morning, midday and evening, two yellow Corporation buses would ferry all and sundry from Fenham Barracks to Blakelaw and back.

On the day following my arrival I was allotted a Married Soldier's Quarters in one of the antiquated Fenham Blocks, but it was in such a bad state that we turned it down and asked for a cleaner one. Unfortunately there was absolutely nothing else and i eventually finished up with a posting to RPO Stockbridge in Hampshire, 9 miles from Winchester. Thus began a long and happy association with this part of the world.

The Pay Office at Stockbridge (which dealt with Parachute Regiment and RAC accounts) was an ex-wartime US Military Hospital which had dealt with the overflow from D-Day - in fact the training section was housed in the former operating theatre! Two hard uphill miles from the village, it was divided into two wings, one for the Pay Office and one for troops' accommodation, connected to each other by covered walkways. It was isolated and bleak, there were no Married Quarters, but the Sgts Mess was friendly and cosy and the work not too exacting. I soon settled in and began to look for family housing. This was more difficult than we had anticipated. The availability of Quarters at Barton Stacey was practically nil and hirings in the district were almost completely non-existent. However, I bought an elderly Ford 8 and scoured the area nightly. I was on the point of giving up when I found this semi-detached house in Twyford (three miles south of Winchester) and, despite the dampness and the antiquities which laughingly had been named as furniture, moved in with Joyce and the girls. We lived a more-or-less settled existence here for a brief period of time and daily I would commute the 12 miles from Twyford to Stockbridge in an ancient contraption, often falling apart half way!

October 1958 saw a flash crisis in Jordan and I was posted overnight to HQ 2 Infantry Brigade Group at Crownhill Fort in Plymouth. The urgency was so great that I only had time to get my kit together, throw it in the boot of the car (yes, another relic, this time a clapped-out old Hillman Minx) and hit the road.
It took most of the day to reach Plymouth and I reported into Crownhill Fort as instructed. It was a forbidding looking piece of architecture, but held a lovely panoramic view of the Hoe and the southwest Devon coastline. The interior of the fort consisted of a small barrack square surrounded by Offices, so there was no actual living accommodation in the Fort. This was in Seaton Barracks on the other side of the main Plymouth-Yeverton road.

I spent the night in a tiny cubicle in the Sergeants Mess Annexe and next day got down to business - issue and fittings of the latest web equipment, lots of unpleasant 'jabs', documentation and a hundred other little jobs that needed to be done. I learnt that the 'Brigade Group' (which was still a fairly new idea in the conception of Infantry formations) had been enlarged to twice its strength for this emergency and many were still being posted in. It was also quite interesting to note that as soon as the words "Active Service" were mentioned, many of the originals suddenly appeared in front of the Medical Officer with hitherto undisclosed diseases and found themselves medically posted out!

As the weeks went by, so the urgency of the move began to slacken off. Within weeks it went from four hours notice to seven days. After a month the whole situation changed and the whole thing collapsed. Nobody however, was posted back to their previous Unit and a Brigade Group became an established part of the British Army.

Several of us now took the opportunity to apply for a Quarter and we all got one in Granby Barracks, Devonport, just across the Tamar from Cornwall, but still within easy commutable distance from Crownhill.

I was allocated an ancient building containing a very smart, modernised flat (nicknamed the "Dream Flat") and I brought Joyce and my children down from Twyford thankfully. We only stayed in the flat for about four months as it was really unsuitable for young children. I applied for, and got, a more modern three bedroom terraced house in 'I' Block. This was an improvement, as it lay away from the main road and adjoined Devonport Park - ideal for the children as it was away from the turmoil of Devonport traffic which can be very hectic (especially in the summer).

We settled down very well and thoroughly enjoyed our stay in the West Country. Joyce's sister Joan and her family lived near Penzance (which was about two hours away by car) and we visited them frequently. We also managed to visit Mother-in-Law in the north and my sister in Kent. By now my 'bangers' were beginning to improve somewhat, although I was sometimes caught out with a lame duck. Anne and Lynn started school and progressed very well. We all enjoyed life in Plymouth for a couple of years and I was really tempted to settle down there. Eventually the 'Brass Hats' in Whitehall decided to disband our Brigade Group and put it into suspended animation, which meant postings all round.

After a lot of chipping and nagging at Major Walsh, the Staff Paymaster, he managed to persuade RAPC Records to give me a Far East posting - a trip I had always wanted. They came up with a Unit Pay Clerk post with 656 Light Aircraft Squadron Army Air Corps in Kuala Lumpur. Unfortunately a wheel come off somewhere along it the line and it was changed to 3 Coy RASC in Ipoh, northern Malaya - my second RASC Company. The news filled us all with excitement, as so far in my 22 years Army service I had never been beyond Europe and I had heard so much about the Far East in conversations round the bar that I was dying to sample this new way of life.

After all the necessary preliminaries i.e. inoculations, MFO boxes, embarkation leave, including the loss and subsequent recovery of a suitcase containing all of our certificates and passports etc., we left Ryton on December 12th and entrained for London.

After reporting in at London Assembly Centre that evening, we were shunted off to RAF Hendon by coach. Next day we left for the airport and Stansted, but halfway there the fog closed down and we were forced to return to Hendon. No break in the weather seemed likely and once again the coach left, this time for Gatwick Airport where all was well.

After a quick meal we climbed aboard our chartered British Eagle Britannia aircraft and, as darkness covered London, we were on our way through the night skies.

We crossed the Alps at around midnight and made good time to our first stop - Istanbul. The monsoon season made Bombay seem like an oven - especially after leaving the English winter.

It seemed as though we had been in the cramped confinement of the plane for weeks when we finally put our wheels down on the tarmac of Paya Lebang Airport, Singapore. The children had been as good as gold all the way (I think they enjoyed the trip), but unfortunately the same could not have been said for Joyce - she had been airsick for nearly all of the journey.

Chapter 10
A FIRST TASTE OF THE ORIENT

The door of the aircraft opened and we deplaned into the oven of the Tropics. The strong odour of curry, durian fruit, humans and heat struck us forcibly and thereafter typified the scents of the Orient.

Singapore was commencing its daily routine and we eventually passed through Customs and Immigration around 10 a.m. Of course this island was no longer part of the British Empire, but the traditions and ways of Queen Victoria still seemed to cling. We were picked up by Army bus and deposited in various hostels around the island. Our family was allocated in the Savoy in a refreshingly beautiful part of the suburbs and, after a much needed bath, rest and meal, were picked up at dusk and taken to the railway station for the journey north. We were given two adjoining sleeping compartments (complete with mosquito net and ceiling fan) and slept soundly as the train

[TEXT ENDS]

EPILOGUE

Sadly Dad never progressed his memoirs beyond this point as he died from cancer on 15 April 1981, aged 58.

I can only hope that in the intervening years before his death he was too busy enjoying himself and never felt the need to update them as he did not expect to die so early. He finished his tour of Japan in 1978 having thoroughly enjoyed the experience of working in the British Embassy where he met and made (as usual!) many friends. On their return to the UK they lived and worked in Winchester until they moved to Poole where he died. Mum still lives here and is as active as she ever was.

He is missed every day by us all and his humour, artistic and musical skills and even certain uncanny physical traits appear to have lived on in his grandchildren, most of whom he never met.

I am sure all the family are grateful to his grandson - Murray Thomson - for finally rescuing the hand written/typed, dog-eared original version of these memoirs and painstakingly putting them together in this book so that we can all share a tangible and lasting memory of a truly decent human being whose kindness, generosity and great sense of humour gave us all many long lasting memories.

Anne Thomson
October 2011